Best
wishes,
Steve
Trachtenberg

THINKING

OUT

LOUD

STEPHEN JOEL TRACHTENBERG

AMERICAN COUNCIL
ON EDUCATION
Series on Higher Education
ORYX PRESS
1998

Copyright © 1998
by American Council on Education
and The Oryx Press

Published by The Oryx Press
4041 North Central at Indian School Road
Phoenix, AZ 85012-3397

Published simultaneously in Canada

Printed and Bound in the United States of America

∞ The paper used in this publication meets the minimum requirements of
American National Standard for Information Science—Permanence of Paper
for Printed Library Materials, ANSI Z39.48, 1984.

THIS BOOK IS DEDICATED TO ALL THE MEMBERS OF
THE GEORGE WASHINGTON UNIVERSITY COMMUNITY,
WHO LARGELY INSPIRED AND GRACIOUSLY LISTENED TO
MANY OF THE OBSERVATIONS HEREIN PROVIDED.

CONTENTS

ix PREFACE

3 TEACHING EFFECTIVENESS
   AND THE NEED FOR ACADEMIC CHANGE
   Remarks at the Columbian College Faculty Symposium,
   The George Washington University, March 31, 1989

11 SEARCHING FOR PERSPECTIVE
    IN A DE-CONTROLLED WORLD
    Keynote address at the annual meeting of Phi Beta Kappa's
    D.C. Alpha Chapter, Washington, D.C., April 21, 1990

19 SHORT TAKES I
    College Costs and Benefits, Higher Education and Jobs,
    Academic Productivity, Business and Education, Education
    and the Economy, Marketing Higher Education

29 LESSONS FROM HUMANITIES 101
    Remarks at the inaugural luncheon of Phi Beta Kappa,
    Washington, D.C., May 10, 1991

37 PRODUCTIVITY AND THE ACADEMIC "BUSINESS"
    Adapted from an article in Productivity and Higher Education:
    Improving the Effectiveness of Faculty, Facilities, and Financial
    Resources *(Peterson's Guides, 1992)*

45 SHORT TAKES II
    The Goals of Higher Education

53 WHY IT MATTERS HOW WE CUT THE CAKE
    Graduation speech at the Sidwell Friends School,
    Washington, D.C., June 11, 1993

59 THE IMPORTANCE OF ANCIENT HISTORY
    Remarks at the Columbia University Convocation,
    New York City, August 31, 1993

65 THE DEATH AND REBIRTH OF EMPATHY
Article in Trusteeship *(Association of Governing Boards of Universities and Colleges), September/October 1994*

73 SHORT TAKES III
Administration and Governance, The Role of Students, The Role of Faculty Members, Reassessing Tenure

83 THE "OUTSIDER INSIDER" EXPERIENCE
Remarks to the high school student class of Operation Understanding, Washington, D.C., May 30, 1995

87 GW AT 175: THE PROGRESS
OF AN ADAPTIVE UNIVERSITY
Remarks to the Newcomen Society of the United States, Washington, D.C., November 30, 1995

95 A VISION FOR THE REFORM OF HIGHER EDUCATION
Remarks at the annual meeting of the Fund for the Improvement of Postsecondary Education, Washington, D.C., October 26, 1996

103 SHORT TAKES IV
International Perspectives, W(h)ither the Humanities? Education and Technology, Education Before College, Educational Opportunity

115 THE CONSEQUENCES OF "THINKING MARKETABILITY"
Remarks at a seminar of the Institute for Educational Leadership, Washington, D.C., March 21, 1997

121 WHAT I LEARNED FROM MY SON
WHO JUST GRADUATED FROM COLUMBIA
Remarks at the annual dinner meeting of the Columbia College Club of Washington, D.C., June 10, 1997

129 THE POWER IN WASHINGTON
COMES FROM A SURPRISING SOURCE!
Keynote address at the "Presidential Classroom for Young Americans" seminar, Washington, D.C., February 1, 1998

135 NOTES & CREDITS

PREFACE

There's something kind of humbling—almost unnerving—about rummaging around in a decade's worth of one's collected expatiations, especially on a subject as important as American higher education. And while the exercise also can be fun, it inevitably generates some rather pointed questions: "Did I really say *that*? What *was* I thinking?" And then, suddenly, the neurons reconnect and the realization springs readily to mind: "*Of course* I said that. And I can remember *very well* what I was thinking . . . although perhaps I could have put that one little point over there a bit more, shall we say, *delicately*."

In any case, the experience of assembling this collection of speeches, articles, and "short takes" from the first 10 years of my presidency at The George Washington University has provided, at least for me, a reassuring sense of what this administrator has judged to be the central problems and opportunities for higher education and, indeed, for those who wish it well. If we've got the problems identified, after all, we're probably moving along on the right track—although, I will be the first to concede, that's not quite the same thing as pulling into the station.

As the reader will note, certain themes tend to reappear throughout this "tome." And it's interesting to me that, despite the march of time and all the changes we have seen in our academic institutions and the world in general, some of the major issues we were dealing with in the late 1980s still seem to be very much with us as we near the end of the '90s. I leave it to others to determine precisely what that means.

Perhaps it's an indication of how *prescient* we were back in the '80s as we demonstrated our ability to identify serious challenges that not only were confronting us *then*, but that would continue to test both the academic community and American society through the end of the current millennium and beyond. I sincerely hope it does *not* mean that the problems have persisted because we have failed to address them adequately. But I must confess: Part of me thinks there may well be something to that last notion.

As a long-time university president, my greatest interest—and the context for much of what you are about to read—is the welfare of higher education as a whole, and of my own university in particular. I am quite passionate about this, and I think it goes to the core of what academic administration should be about: We must all work hard to protect, nourish, and strengthen our universities and colleges because their success is crucial to the future of our nation and our own lives. I know that may sound like a cliché, but you do have to wonder sometimes whether the message has been received.

All around me I find that, while my own university seems to be doing well, the university as a collective institution is under assault—as it has been, in fact, for years. Essentially that is because people are angry. Now more than ever, they want access to higher education for themselves and their children—nay, they *insist* on having access—but as they have come to know only too well, higher education is *expensive*.

So there we have what is probably Issue No. 1 for American universities and colleges, now and for the foreseeable future: *Money!* Money to enroll in courses, money to pay the people who work in the institutions, money to subsidize the education of people who can't afford it themselves, money to repair the roof and install the computer network, money to pay your bills and put in the bank from the paycheck you earn because of the college degree you acquired. You will find frequent references to these matters on the following pages (which, by the way, I have organized more or less in chronological order so that you may consider the evolution, if not the constancy, of my thinking).

Besides all the attention to financial issues, you will see me dwelling on questions of content and process. What, after all, is this thing called *higher learning*? What courses of study, what knowledge, what skills, and what perspectives should we be offering to our students in exchange for their time and their (or their parents') hard-earned tuition payments? Those are age-old questions, to be sure, but ask around and you may discover that the jury is still out. The humanities? The classics? The liberal arts? All well and good, perhaps, but what about vocational training and "marketable skills" and the graduate's ability to earn a living? We who would teach in and oversee the administration of our colleges and universities had better come up with the goods on that one, or someone else surely will.

And while we are on the subject of teaching: How important is it in the academic scheme of things? Increasingly, the answer we get from the folks *out there*, beyond the campus, is that teaching is more important than just about everything else. Gone are the days when research was king. Undergraduates, especially, demand an emphasis on good teaching. What faculty members do in the laboratory or in the library for their own professional knowledge and advancement may still be an essential part of what higher education is all about, just as those activities may still be vital in helping professors stay current in their academic specialties. Students may understand that, but they also want to interact with faculty members who know *how to teach*, who make themselves available after class, and who generally try to do their best for the "customers" who, after all, help pay their salaries.

Those are among the broad issues I felt compelled to address in the essays and speeches that I tapped for this compilation. As you would expect, they explore a range of other ideas about higher education—such as academic tenure, affirmative action, faculty productivity, information technology, and "shared governance." All in all, I've tried to make this volume fairly representative of my writing and speechmaking during the past 10 years. Notice that while I start off in 1989 with an exposition on teaching, I end up in 1998 with an acknowledgement of the power that young people exert in American life today. It's a case, I submit, of coming full circle.

To be sure, I devote considerable attention in these pages to *problems* and *criticisms*, but you should know that I am basically an *optimist* at heart. For while American higher education clearly needs to be reformed, I have no doubt that it has the people and the capacity to make the right changes.

Speaking of changes, I should mention an incidental point: As I reviewed the original texts and transcripts of the works in this volume, I found a number of places where I wished I'd said or written things somewhat differently. So now, possessing the rare luxury of a second shot, I have decided to exercise an editor's prerogative and have made minor refinements and other adjustments where I thought they might help to convey my thoughts more effectively. Substantively, though, you still have the essence of the originals.

—*Stephen Joel Trachtenberg*

THINKING

OUT

LOUD

1 9 8 9

TEACHING EFFECTIVENESS AND THE NEED FOR ACADEMIC CHANGE

REMARKS AT THE COLUMBIAN COLLEGE FACULTY SYMPOSIUM,
THE GEORGE WASHINGTON UNIVERSITY, MARCH 31, 1989

Many years ago I began to observe that university presidents don't usually add to their popularity when they attempt to "meddle" in academic matters. The feeling at many institutions is that the poor man or woman in the head office may be good enough to do a bit of fund raising and public relations—and, of course, to deal with the university budget. But as for matters of curriculum, teaching, and research . . . well, those should be left to people who are actually qualified to discuss them.

That being so often the attitude, it's not only an honor but a pleasure to know that The George Washington University is the exception that proves the rule. Folks around here tend to underrate both themselves and their institution.

Indeed, my own past experiences at such places as Columbia, Yale, Harvard, Oxford, and Boston Universities, as well as the University of Hartford—not to mention in countless visits to other institutions—give me the confidence to say that GW has some very special characteristics that look more special as time goes on, not only here but also beyond our walls.

We all have the pain (or privilege) of living at a time when the stone walls surrounding *Alma Mater* have turned to glass, and the cloistered academy has become a goldfish bowl. What were once the deepest secrets of academe—secrets because the public felt no strong desire to figure them out—are now openly discussed in the news media, corporate boardrooms, and legislative hearings (both in the states and in Congress), not to mention in barbershops and hair salons. The motivation for this great new public interest is obvious: The tuition we must charge to keep our institutions healthy has been widely declared to be a national problem.

This new concern, over both what people have to pay for higher education and what they receive in return, has been intensified by other familiar developments on the economic front. When a family's home in a reasonable suburb used to cost $50,000, many people felt that another $5,000 to $8,000 a year for college tuition, room, and board was bearable. But now, when the home is much more likely to cost $250,000 or more—demanding a two-earner family plus additional funds from parents or relatives for the down payment—the notion that a family must find an additional $20,000 a year for a child's college education is *no laughing matter.*

So here we are—and I say "we" because I, like you, am a GW faculty member . . . here we are, trying to live up to the ideals that led us into the academic world in the first place (ideals that had a lot more to do with the pleasure of learning and teaching than any desire to accumulate wealth), only to find that we are being examined like some business or government office that's suspected of cheating its clients and wasting their money.

It's not a climate I relish, and it's not simply going to go away. *Because* it is so connected with other economic and cultural trends, some of them global rather than national, it's a climate with which we are going to have to learn how to cope. And frankly, I'd rather try coping with it from the vantage point of GW than from that offered by any other institution in the United States.

The topic for this discussion, "Teaching Effectiveness," is a slogan that many see as the focal point for most of the current debate about American higher education. All the other alleged abuses by colleges and universities, assert our critics as they sign new publishing contracts, cannot be justified or explained away by an emphasis on good teaching. On the contrary, they say, academe's costly abuses *negate* the teaching function, and increasingly push it to the back burner.

Ours being a symposium not graced by media representatives, we could probably spend an hour or two just exchanging anecdotes about the extent to which a strong commitment to teaching wasn't even discussed in the course of our own graduate education. As the saying used to go: "You can pick all that up after you've received your degree and obtained your first job." Back then, a focus on teaching may have seemed appropriate for those getting ready to instruct third-graders or high school students. But for much of academe, especially those parts of it with a seeming interest in "quality," that did not include kowtowing to the attention spans of adolescents.

A campus would tolerate the eccentricities of dear old Professor Schmidlap, whose definitive book on Sanskrit epigraphy was going into its third edition and whose lectures, recited in a barely audible drone from notes so old they were falling apart, had long ago eclipsed Nembutal as a soporific. The same campus would have no compunction about denying tenure to—that is, dismissing—young Professor Vim-'n'-Vigor, whose lectures drew higher attendance than *Gone With the Wind*, but whose book hadn't quite reached the point at which it could be submitted for publication.

That, of course, was the world immediately following World War II, and it was a less-than-democratic world in which those earning college degrees had, almost by definition, received an elitist or semi-elitist education. Their first employers could assume they had mastered the arts of reading, writing, and understanding; that they could read, if not also speak, one or two foreign languages, and that they knew something about history.

But that was *then*. For all kinds of good reasons, America soon became a nation in which more and more money began pouring into our colleges and universities, while the salaries of teachers and staff members rose only gradually. We were providing a cornucopia of benefits at a relatively low cost. Four years of college and some postgraduate training could be obtained at a price that most middle-class Americans could afford. State colleges and community colleges extended comparable privileges to those whose incomes fell below middle-class levels. Significantly, it was not until the costs of higher education began to increase steeply, even as personal-income levels began to suffer a net decline, that critical evaluations of teaching effectiveness seemed to become a national obsession.

That said, what can we academicians expect in the next few years? I would offer the following observations:

Observation No. 1: Across the nation, people who work in higher education will start to experience the process traditionally referred to as "going back to the drawing board."

It's easy to forget how recently American universities took the form in which we know them today. Toward the end of the 19th century, teaching was still their primary mission. Many institutions that today are called universities were still known then as colleges. The land-grant origins of the public universities could be seen in their curricula, which in turn were directly related to the economic needs of the regions in which they were located. Meanwhile, private universities, including those with long and distinguished histories, were still places that regarded the teaching of ethics, usually with religious overtones, as one of their important functions.

All of that changed, of course, when American universities "went to school" in Germany. In the systematic Prussian manner, higher education institutions in the German Empire had been organized as primary contributors to the power of an industrialized state that was rapidly outstripping its European competitors in technological advancement—and, therefore, in political, military, and economic power. The German system's research orientation, along with its focus on awarding postgraduate degrees of unimpeachable respectability, began to replace America's homegrown varieties of higher education—a process not fully completed until soon after World War II.

The idea that something might have been lost as well as gained in this process has always been a background theme when Americans have assessed their universities. There's long been a lingering suspicion that the true genius of higher education in this country may have been diverted by the German model. That belief has grown lately as Americans have become acquainted with Japan's education system, where the "heavy work" gets done in elementary school and high school; Japanese universities, meanwhile, are regarded—relatively speaking—as vacation spots for those preparing to enter the heart of the national economy.

So the idea of an approaching "return to the drawing board" for American academics is less absurd than we might have been inclined to feel, say, 10 years ago. And when the reassessment comes, it will no doubt have a lot to do with teaching effectiveness. We are a society in shock as we discover and rediscover that our desperate need for skilled, trained, and trainable workers is *not* being met by the combined resources of our primary, secondary, and postsecondary public *and* private education systems. The structure is vast, but the results so far are not commensurately impressive.

Every time an employer meets someone with a postsecondary degree who cannot make it from the left side of a memo to the right-hand margin without committing a serious grammatical and/or spelling error, the shock begins all over again: 18 or 19 years of education, costing hundreds of thousands of dollars for this one individual, have failed to produce an employee whose simplest written communications can be forwarded without third-party intervention (be it careful proofreading by someone over the age of 40 or the use of "spell check" software on a secretary's word processor).

But the issue of teaching effectiveness cannot be considered in isolation. Every other part of our educational structure will need to change as well. Which leads me to . . .

Observation No. 2: Those who used to be considered our "super" teachers will be seen, increasingly, as more or less "ordinary" teachers—albeit the ones who deserve their salaries and reasonably secure jobs.

Super teachers not only know what's going on in their students' minds but also are keenly aware of what's going on outside the academic walls. Whether they call what they do reading or research, whether it takes place in the university library or the public library, they will stay on top of "their" subjects while keeping up with a lot of other subjects as well. They also will succeed in integrating this entire body of knowledge in the classroom. Super teachers may indeed publish books and articles, even highly regarded ones. But those works, which typically emerge as a labor of love, often begin when the teacher converts complicated subject matter into more digestible sequences for the benefit of students.

There is little discomfort (among honest people) when a super teacher *doesn't* have a huge publication record. His or her equivalent of a 16-hour day is all too obvious to colleagues for whom a comparable length of time, spent in the stacks of a major research library, isn't something they exactly look forward to.

There is an important wrinkle in all of this. As super teachers become more the expected norm, those now regarded as "normal" may find themselves regarded increasingly as "substandard." But that's the price of the omelette known as Revolution—which, as was first observed in the Stone Age, can't be carried out without breaking some eggs.

I began this piece by suggesting that The George Washington University is the exception that proves the rule. If I were presiding over a more typical university while all these criticisms of higher education were being bandied about in the media, I would be a very nervous person. But consider—

Observation No. 3: As President of GW, rather than of a more typical university, I'm a lot more tranquil than my own personal history of nervousness might ever give me reason to expect.

When Columbian College addresses the issue of teaching effectiveness in a meeting like this, and when it actually invites the university president to initiate the discussion, I know that what we have here in Foggy Bottom is a truly functional institution that won't have to relearn how to survive the kind of storms we see building on the horizon. At a time when doing nothing amounts to a retreat, Columbian College and The George Washington University have chosen the direction I myself prefer: *forward.*

1 9 9 0

SEARCHING FOR PERSPECTIVE IN A DE-CONTROLLED WORLD

KEYNOTE ADDRESS AT THE ANNUAL MEETING OF PHI BETA KAPPA'S
D.C. ALPHA CHAPTER, WASHINGTON, D.C., APRIL 21, 1990

I'd like to talk about the humanities, the social sciences, and the natural sciences, and how those three aspects of what we usually call the "arts and sciences" relate to society in general as we approach the end of the 20th century.

This is not a topic that posed many problems when I was an undergraduate in the 1950s. Back then, the humanities—meaning written texts from the Bible and Homer to Dostoevsky, Nietzsche, and Freud— were what you had to study for at least two years, along with separate one-semester courses on music and the fine arts. The social and behavioral sciences were mostly optional parts of the undergraduate curriculum, and still regarded at the time as a little flaky and uncontrolled. Meanwhile, the natural sciences—which were neatly divided into chemistry, physics, zoology, astronomy, and geology—typically generated two difficult electives that many students delayed taking until their junior or senior year . . . and didn't much care for even then!

In that relatively simple environment, few instructors of Introductory Humanities bothered to inform us that paintings, poems, statues, novels, and musical works had ever been created in East Asia or West Africa or pre-Columbian America. That was something you could find out for yourself if you registered for the appropriate electives, like Oriental Humanities or Anthropology 101 or Art History.

Back then, no one imagined that a Nobel Prize-winning chemist could be someone who almost never entered a laboratory but did his work while closeted with a computer (I'm referring here to Dr. Roald Hoffman of Cornell, with whom I graduated from Columbia in 1959). And it would have sounded like pure fantasy to talk about theoretical astronomers who referred to the universe as made up of "mind stuff."

Back in the '50s, some of the most dramatic experimental proofs of Einsteinian physics were unavailable. No one had yet flown an atomic clock several times around the earth in a high-speed jet, successfully demonstrating that when it landed it was milliseconds behind the synchronized control clock that hadn't budged from its spot near the runway. No one had yet thought of exploiting a complete solar eclipse to show that starlight *is* bent by the sun's gravitation on its way to Earth. No one had yet demonstrated on an unshakable statistical basis that a single suicide, when reported in the newspaper, is followed by a wave of others.

And in a world fixated on Thor Heyerdahl and his raft Kon-Tiki as he struggled to show that pre-Columbian societies had been influenced—or at least influenceable—by the cultures of Southeast Asia, no one paid much attention to such known cross-cultural phenomena as the Roman mirrors found in Chinese tombs of the Han Dynasty; the Greek-influenced Buddhist sculptures of the earliest centuries A.D.; the coconuts that found their way to northern Europe during the Middle Ages and were promptly mounted in gold and silver holders as drinking cups for royalty and nobility; the statuette of Buddha found in a Viking tomb; the extraordinary Afro-Portuguese ivories of the 15th and 16th centuries; the Benin bronzes of West Africa that were collected by Europeans as early as the first quarter of the 18th century; or the African sculptures that so strongly influenced Picasso and other artists of the early 20th century.

No—back then, the humanities meant works created in the West, the social sciences meant mostly behavioral psychology, and the natural sciences meant clearly separable disciplines whose interdepartmental aspects were discussed, by appropriately qualified researchers, only at the postgraduate level. Back then, moreover, it looked and felt as if those neat definitions would endure forever and ever.

Since then, of course, the world of knowledge has exploded in all directions! How desperately we now run, especially within our universities and four-year colleges, to catch up with the consequences of that intellectual Big Bang! And how frenzied have become some of the voices that warn us of an enormous "new ignorance" in which politicized college curricula are aimed—or flung—at students who are more likely to push a button on audio-visual equipment than to crack a book or read a newspaper.

Indeed, I would suggest that in the world of ideas, including both academic life and high culture in general, people are actually panicking in the face of new challenges to the old agreed-upon truths and "obvious" realities. Holding one's tongue is certainly not the problem; all tongues are wagging, all fingers are typing, all publications are publishing, and all screens are glowing as the charges fly back and forth among every gender, ethnic group, and ideological position.

Meanwhile, an increasingly bewildered general public struggles to understand how last month's good news about cancer or cholesterol or global warming, for example, can sometimes be entirely contradicted and reversed in a matter of weeks.

Concealment is no longer our problem; revelation is. Only persons of paranoid disposition still suspect that all physicians, all lawyers, or even all businessmen are capable of sinister conspiracies aimed at depriving and defrauding the human race. I deliberately except top government officials from that list because their conspiracies have been all too copiously and sometimes tragically documented.

No, the problem today, at least for the general public, is how to evaluate the bona fides or experimental accuracy of distinguished scientists from some of our most prestigious institutions when they present thoroughly opposite findings on the same subject. If panic isn't the appropriate response to that, what is?

Let me try to cast a little light on the subject by presenting a somewhat radical hypothesis. My thought is that in the second half of the 20th century we have so dramatically revised our sense of time, space, and human culture that the gulf between a Stone Age tribe and America in 1950 is narrower than the one between America in 1950 and America today.

Consider our sense of time. When we aren't doing work that we actually hate, most of us no longer experience the type of boredom, which the French have always called *ennui*, that was so common among even young people in the 1950s—the sense of having absolutely nothing to do, no one to get in touch with, nothing worth exploring; the sense of time as an oppressing burden, with the slow ticking of a clock as the epitome of personal emptiness. Today, in contrast, the presence of so many distractions and data sources, often accessible at the push of a button, allows us to move instantaneously from one set of brand-new phenomena to another, to extend consciousness as far and as fast as electricity can reach, and to communicate—again, instantaneously—with other people who in 1950 would have been weeks or even months away from contact.

The same developments have radically eroded our previous sense of space. Miles count for nothing in today's world unless your car breaks down. Communications from outer space can reach Vladivostok as quickly as they can reach Washington, Bangkok, or Cairo. The words and face of a political leader can be studied on a split screen whose other half is running the live coverage of a riot that contradicts everything he or she is saying.

The net impact of all this continues to be a reversal of certain cultural assumptions that stem from the Renaissance, and the restoration of a sense of reality not entirely unlike one that prevailed in Western Europe during the Middle Ages. It was during the Renaissance and the immediately subsequent period, after all, that some of our most central assumptions received their classic formulation. For example:

∽ The visual assumption that there is such a thing as perspective, and that its laws are absolute.

∽ The philosophical assumption that time is divided into equal and unchangeable units.

∽ The cartographical assumption that our planet can be neatly divided, on a two-dimensional surface, into equal units of latitude and longitude.

∽ The literary assumption, resurrected from the ancient Greeks, that every coherent work of prose or poetry must have a clear beginning, middle, and end.

∽ The bibliographical assumption that all human knowledge can be gathered in printed works, which can then be physically stored in many separate places and made available to everyone who knows how to read.

∽ The bureaucratic assumption—epitomized in the work of Richelieu, Linnaeus, and Descartes—that every aspect of life, from government to education to the animal and vegetable species, can be divided into hierarchically arranged departments.

Take geometry. Those who lived in the Middle Ages were certainly not ignorant about geometry; otherwise, how could they have built such enormous cathedrals, only a few of which fell down? They certainly applied geometry to religious experience—as Dante and Aquinas demonstrated, to the dismay of many modern readers. But it took the Renaissance and post-Renaissance periods to suggest that a neat, compartmentalized, ultimately geometrical vision could be applied to every aspect of human life, and that human control (over the environment, over what were then considered the lower classes, and over physical reality itself) could therefore be infinitely extended. Systems of classification developed at that time, and amounting to nothing less than a comprehensive world vision, are still with us today. Pyramids of every conceivable sort continue to be erected for every human purpose imaginable—from schools and business organizations to government, the arts, literature, science, and the determination of who's No. 1 or No. 55 among plumbers, electricians, discus throwers, universities, fast-food restaurants, developers of nuclear and biochemical warfare, and builders of Taj Mahals and Eiffel Towers out of toothpicks, matchbook covers, and Frisbees!

In other words, in the world view we have inherited from the post-Medieval period, compartments are neat, progressions are clear, processes are predictable, and the universe is under mental control (which, in turn, has furthered the long-term human project of getting the universe under our physical control as well).

I would like to suggest now that we have entered a time marked by de-control—a time in which the very instruments with which we seek to establish control interfere with whatever goal they, and we who manipulate them, are trying to attain.

The phenomenon is nothing less than a mega-version of the uncertainty principle that nuclear physicists faced earlier in this century. Back then, you'll remember, using a cloud chamber was the only way of "seeing" a nuclear particle, and what you saw was only where it had been. Attempts to catch it "live" through the use of light were frustrated by the fact that light, in one of its two simultaneous aspects, consists of photons, and that these particles would knock the ones under observation off course.

Something similar is true of an assumption that in 1950 was so obvious that it was never even discussed—the assumption that government could produce certain desirable results by creating a "program" whose "officials" would spend the required money in a logical way that was determined by other "officials" who had previously engaged in a completely rational, objectively perfect process called "planning."

For example, people might well have observed back then that America was developing peacetime nuclear power of a kind so perfectly controlled that it would provide a 100 percent safe source of cheap power for every man, woman, and child in the country. And weren't we protected from our enemies by a defense system so brilliantly monitored that it was 100 percent fail-safe? And wasn't a wonderfully effective pesticide like DDT the perfect solution to the problem of world hunger?

How much more scared, how much less certain, and how much less optimistic we have all become in the intervening years. Even as our world has speeded up—even as it has become so much more contracted and accessible; even as we have extended the eyes, ears, and memories of our computerized control systems from pole to pole and out into space—we have become less certain, less trusting, less hopeful, and less assured about anything except the immediate present in which we live.

I'd sum up the result as a loss of perspective. The ever-changing realities that now swirl around us are like the figures in a Medieval woodcut, which all bear an obvious relationship to each other but aren't located in a "perspectival" landscape or cityscape. Jesus confronts Satan, Lazarus is raised from the dead, a saint is tortured, Daniel looks a lion in the eye, Moses confronts Pharaoh—in the middle of no place in particular. Even the soaring interior of a cathedral, originally so full of painted "special effects" in addition to the stained-glass windows, was designed to disarm and disable the sense of a clear, assured stability in which even the tallest tree had its limits and measurement kept things more or less under control.

We're also living now with a loss of control. Attempts to regain control seem like the obvious solution—the one we have inherited from our progenitors. But such attempts increasingly fail, or raise new problems of control that are even more mind-boggling.

Indeed, the most significant event of recent years, the one most laden with symbolism, may be the failure of the 1990 U.S. Census. With so much high tech at its disposal, so many new tricks for gathering and storing an infinity of data, the government of the United States could not count, to a minimally adequate extent, the population it represents. Measurement itself broke down—and measurement, more than anything else, is fundamental to the very notion of achieving control.

Having said all these things, some of them rather grim, let me end on a hopeful note. The new members of this Alpha Chapter represent a generation of Americans who will somehow have to deal with our new reality in new and unforeseeable ways. It will be your generational task to reconsider the very bases of our culture, our government, and our everyday philosophical assumptions—the ones that help to determine what we are capable of thinking and, therefore, doing.

We may live in a post-Renaissance world, but we also live in a pre-Something-Else world. And when we discover what the Something Else will look like and feel like, no doubt we will think back to you and your work and will say: "They brought us through. What felt at the time like collapse turned out, after all, to be creation. To *them* we owe the fact that we are no longer anxious or panicky, but settled in our new way of life, with which we are reasonably but finally content."

SHORT TAKES I

COLLEGE COSTS AND BENEFITS

In recent years, critics of American colleges and universities have claimed that students and their families aren't getting sufficient value for their money, especially at independent institutions. Such attacks have continued despite the well-known fact that the true cost of education at private universities is significantly greater than the tuition they charge.

At public institutions, the true cost can be eight or nine times the tuition, with the difference being made up by the state. Private universities, meanwhile, have for many years been seeking greater cost-effectiveness and new ways to limit tuition increases. Today there is no corner of most university budgets that has not been examined many times over in search of expenses that can be eliminated or reduced. Indeed, university administrators are sometimes criticized for being overly concerned with finances at the expense of curriculum, teaching effectiveness, and academic research.

Why, then, do colleges and universities continue to be targets for such criticism? One factor, I would suggest, is that so many Americans are now deeply involved with higher education. When something is that important, it is natural to overemphasize shortcomings and underemphasize benefits. As recently as 1939, only 6 percent of all Americans attended higher education institutions for any length of time. Today the percentage is 60 to 70 percent. In our society, universities have become an almost universal fact of life, touching the lives of most of our citizens as they make lifelong personal and career plans.

Critics demand that American universities lower their tuition, but they usually don't acknowledge how that might lead to the elimination of the very student-centered services that distinguish our universities from their European, Asian, and African counterparts.

— "Cost-Conscious Universities Don't Deserve Scapegoat Status,"
in *Connection*, New England Board of Higher Education, Summer 1988

Universities share one serious flaw. They, and their faculty members in particular, distrust anything that smacks too conspicuously of advertising or marketing. At a critical time like the present, when most academic budgets are under such serious pressure that talk of terminating untenured and sometimes tenured faculty has become common, our universities and colleges also share a flaw with American industry—the tendency to spend a lot more on marketing when enrollments (= sales) are booming than when they are in retreat.

That, of course, has long been acknowledged by industry analysts to represent a 180-degree error. Budgetary balance in the academic context must be a balance conducive to the long-term survival and viability of the specific school being *marketed* to its potential students and their families. Resource allocations here must not be cut back without the most serious self-examination.

— "The Difficult Quest for Balance in American Higher Education,"
in *The World & I,* The Washington Times Corporation, December 1991

∾

HIGHER EDUCATION AND JOBS

For some students, the current pattern of worry about jobs and careers may have an unfortunate, narrowing effect—by encouraging them to develop a prematurely "tight focus" on the single field or professional specialization that seems to be offering jobs right now. Hopefully a student's teachers and counselors will encourage him or her to remember how many different jobs and career approaches are now typical in a single person's lifetime. Learning how to learn and how to adapt are two of the most important lessons our undergraduates need to master.

Increasingly, colleges and universities attract students with the promise that the institutions are conduits to employment and rewarding careers. They may boast about their relationships with local and regional employers, and how these give undergraduates a "leg up" toward a good job. They may thump their chests with regard to the effectiveness of their programs in communication, computer science, and reasoning skills. They may describe the benefits resulting from their remedial programs in math and science. But the common denominator that links these self-promotional efforts can be summed up in a single promise: "Those who receive their undergraduate education here are gaining a head start toward a rewarding career."

—Remarks to the National Center for Academic Achievement
and Transfer Panel, Philadelphia, Pa., October 19, 1992

W e're in the middle of a profound redefinition of academic consciousness—one that applies to everyone on the payroll—and it can be summed up in a single sentence: "What we don't earn is what we can't spend." Everyone drawing a salary needs to consider what he or she has done *today* to keep that salary coming. Everyone needs to be aware, from moment to moment, what the institution's "customers," formerly known as its students, want.

—Remarks to the Whitney Center, Hamden, Conn., March 11, 1996

S tep into an American university today and you will find an emphasis on careers that would have seemed unimaginable half a century ago. Back then, students were of course aware that they would have to find their way into a profession of some kind. If the undergraduates 50 years ago were thinking of law school, they tended to take courses in government and political science. If they hoped to go to medical school, their choices were often mandated narrowly to feature chemistry and biology.

But what is so amazing in retrospect is the extent to which "career issues" of this kind were pushed onto the "back burner" of academic considerations.

—Address to the Secretary's Open Forum, U.S. Department
of State, Washington, D.C., November 2, 1997

P rice is one of higher education's top issues. There's terrible confusion between price and cost. People wonder why it costs $5,000 a year at a state university and $20,000 at a private university.

What's marvelous is that private institutions can not only survive but flourish in an environment in which we're selling a service that others down the street are "giving away." But you have to provide value for the money.

—Interview at The George Washington University, February 2, 1998

༠༡

ACADEMIC PRODUCTIVITY

Enhanced academic productivity is the only way in which universities and four-year colleges are going to keep their collective railroad train from jumping the rails and ending up in the kind of fiscal shape that doesn't invite but *mandates* government intervention— probably at the federal level. American institutions of higher education are at the point today, in other words, that the nation's savings and loan associations were at in the late 1980s. What they are doing, how they are doing it, and how they propose to go *on* doing it isn't viable, can't last, and, within a few years, is going to bring about the very thing academicians most fear, which is the kind of "outside intervention" that has little use for traditional academic values and practices.

Where the *academic* side of universities and colleges is concerned, productivity—the amount of teaching provided to student customers in both quantitative and qualitative terms—has not only remained static but has actually declined. Since World War II, weekly hours spent in the classroom or instructional laboratory have declined from 15 to 12 to nine to an increasingly common average of six, while researchers of sufficient status have experienced even more dramatic reductions to three hours or even *zero* hours per week.

Instructional office hours that are actually kept are often experienced by student customers in search of a particular teacher as a crap game with worse odds than you can find in Las Vegas. "Advisement" has become almost a dirty word—a function to be relegated, at many schools, to whoever is currently at the bottom of the academic pecking order. And the whole rickety system—in which the only fiscal component that steadily rises is the one representing salaries and fringe benefits—has been kept tottering along by the widespread use of part-time faculty and teaching assistants. These people provide 40 to 60 percent of the actual instruction at most universities and a somewhat smaller majority of four-year colleges.

Something's got to give. *Something's* got to change. *Some* safety valve needs to be built into our academic system if the pressure cooker—consisting of rising public anger and government demands, especially at the state level—is to be kept from exploding. And that safety valve (although I'm not supposed to mention it) is the one provided by fully available, fully accessible, easily mastered modern technology.

But easy as these resources are to master, they require a serious commitment if they are to be effectively and productively *used.* They also are likely to bring about a major readjustment in the way our institutions of higher education now function.

But technological resources do not favor the slow and cumbersome arrangements in which the smallest academic proposal for doing things differently has to work its way, often over a period of years, from the individual level to the department to the division to the vice president to the president to the board of trustees. Official approval is required at each stage, and the proposal may well be "sent back" several times for restructuring and reassessment. What the resources *do* favor is rapid coordination among all who are likely to benefit from them if they are used creatively.

—Remarks at the "Outlook 2010" Conference,
Fairfax County Public Schools, McLean, Va., April 18, 1990

෴

BUSINESS AND EDUCATION

Back in the not-so-good old days, when those working in higher education felt about business the way folks in a horror movie do about the neighborhood vampire, one of their complaints was that business people were grossly motivated only by efficiency, also known as the quest for profits. But in the process of turning business into a bugaboo, those working in higher education were also able to elevate *inefficiency* into a positive virtue.

American higher education became one of the very few enclaves in world history of which it could be said that the people in it were able to do *whatever they wanted.* "Businesslike efficiency" continued to be a no-no, even as the waters of the national economy turned cooler, then colder, then icy. And in a particularly insidious development, the administrative side of many universities and colleges learned to ape the academic side when it came to looseness of structure and a lack of interest in the relationship between money spent and practical results obtained. Higher education sowed the wind of cheerful inefficiency; today it is reaping a whirlwind of growing public distrust and fiscal crisis. Here's a suggestion: Let's get academic and business leaders together to determine (a) what higher education institutions must now do to achieve fiscal stability, and (b) how to accomplish that in ways that also serve the national economic interest.

Like it or not, American businesses need American higher education, and corporate leaders must serve as guarantors to the public that higher education has put its spending practices into reasonable alignment with its productivity.

Even as business people master the art of working with colleges and universities to serve their own best interests—and the nation's—they are also going to have to become a lot shrewder and a lot more demanding about what gets done with the money they contribute. Academic institutions need to bid for contributions—and need to learn the fine art of making those bids highly competitive. They are also going to have to master the fine art of reporting on how those funds have been spent—in reports that can actually stand up, if necessary, to the most unexpected of audits and critiques.

—Remarks at *The New York Times* Presidents Forum,
New York City, November 22, 1991

∾

EDUCATION AND THE ECONOMY

A merican higher education *may* be as seriously defective and as out-of-whack-with-reality as its critics allege. But right now it is, and into the foreseeable future will be, the only thing standing between this nation and a really *serious* economic decline. And in a world where nations other than our own are usually becoming *more* diverse and heterogeneous—a world, for example, in which West Germans are finding their East German "brothers" only somewhat less alien than their Turkish immigrants—we must also note that American higher education, subjected to such furious fire by its domestic critics, is often the subject of international admiration and emulation. Defective?—maybe. Essential?—certainly.

—Remarks at the "Outlook 2010" Conference,
Fairfax County Public Schools, McLean, Va., April 18, 1990

൬

MARKETING HIGHER EDUCATION

Once high school seniors experience the "bidding process" through which colleges and universities seek to attract *some* of them, higher education's mystique is effectively dissolved. The contrary principle also applies: Colleges making no attempts to attract talented applicants are likely to be perceived as probably (a) overcrowded and/or (b) absurdly cheap and/or (c) unable, for one reason or another, to really compete with "big bucks."

—Remarks to the National Center for Academic Achievement
and Transfer Panel, Philadelphia, Pa., October 19, 1992

1991

LESSONS FROM HUMANITIES 101

REMARKS AT THE INAUGURAL LUNCHEON OF PHI BETA KAPPA,
WASHINGTON, D.C., MAY 10, 1991

A frequent explanation for the decline of literacy among people who have been to college—even among those who have gone on, apparently, to receive graduate degrees—is that we are living in a predominantly visual age, and that television in particular has "swept all before it." Indeed, many serious people are now willing to consider the hypothesis that prolonged exposure to TV alters neurological functioning and acquires an addictive and hypnotic power over the human mind—a power that is difficult to reverse and that soon requires the medium's perpetual presence. As Madison Avenue pundits observed long ago, in a statement they regarded as a truism rather than an insight: "People don't watch television. They have it on." All household and family activities are conducted with one eye, so to speak, "on the set," and with its visual and auditory emanations occupying a corner of everybody's consciousness for 36 or 40 or even 45 hours a week. And each morning, at work or at school, much of the conversation is about "what was on last night" and "What did you think of it?"

This ubiquitous electronic intruder exercises tutorial as well as distractive power over the human mind. It is a spectacular catalyst of words and behaviors that can be described as "acting out." Once TV has done its work, all of the other electronic and print media function—often in spite of themselves—as supplementary catalysts. Soon, even those pleading for moderation and "a middle way" find themselves feeding the huge bonfire of nationwide and/or international concern, as the epidemic feeling spreads that so many voices must signify Such Great Importance.

Meanwhile, as always tends to be the case when enormous numbers of people get involved in a dispute, the issues become simplified into a kind of mental shorthand that features a few vivid phrases and quotations and, in so visual an age, a few apparently defining images. These easy-to-remember simplifications tend to be accompanied, naturally enough, by an Armageddon-like mentality in which you choose your side, with whatever misgivings, and saunter into battle to see whether yours or the wicked "other side" can capture the human soul.

Such has been the recent conflict, at least as the media and most Americans see it, over the nature of the undergraduate curriculum in our colleges and universities. On one side are the proponents of Western tradition as the bedrock of responsible collegiate education. On the other side are those who insist that the study of diverse non-Western experiences is just as important, a lot more relevant, and therefore more pedagogically effective when it comes to educating "people of color."

And there is our Manichean Struggle of the Year: Proponents of uniformity are ranged, in the manner of both the men and the gods of the *Iliad*, against their opposite numbers, who are proponents of diversity. We needn't do much research to find the associated imagery—white male professors, no doubt middle-aged, in the Harris Tweed jackets they inherited from their grandfathers, versus young and vigorously protesting "people of color" and their Caucasian sympathizers, who are as likely to be female as male.

"You're totally obsolete!" cries the latter group with one voice as the battle is joined. "You've got nothing on your side but the politics of injustice!"

To which their opponents reply (after removing briar pipes from clenched teeth): "You think Malcolm X is as good as Dante, Shakespeare, and Tolstoy! What you don't know about politics would fill a good-sized library—and does."

And after that, it's the National Association of Scholars versus the entire Third World, and may the best cardboard cutouts win the day! Watching and listening as caricatures like those fill the air whenever the issues of diversity, multiculturalism, and the Western "canon" are . . . dare I even say it? . . . *under discussion* has been especially disheartening to me. I've seen similar conflicts all too many times, and I know that what is coming next is the Tedium Phase, in which the whole debate has been heard and seen once too often. At that point, of course, the media and their vast modern audiences will turn their attention to some newer battle that looks even juicier. And when that happens rather suddenly, at some point in the coming weeks, our universities and colleges will find themselves left to curricular squabbling, which will no doubt drag on forever on a case-by-case, school-by-school basis.

But let us look at the true "basics" of this particular Armageddon through nonpolemical eyes. We can begin with the spring issue of the National Academy of Scholars' newsletter, *NAS Update*, in which the organization's president, Stephen H. Balch, says the following:

"There is, of course, an obviously disingenuous character to the multiculturalist argument. Few academic multiculturalists have any interest in guaranteeing a place in the curriculum for Avicenna, Sun Tzu, Lady Murasaki, or Tagore. They focus on figures like Frantz Fanon, Rigoberta Menchu, and Alice Walker, who, though 'people of color,' are entirely Western in voice and outlook. What is desired is not cultural 'otherness,' but cultural insurgency—employing radical feminism, Marxism, nationalism, or some other uniquely Western school of thought to expose liberal institutions to a devastating critique."

Balch goes on to argue that the domination of multiculturalist thinking by Western categories and assumptions is typical of the spectacular influence that the West has had on all other cultures, and that the West's "present ascendancy rests on the success of its material, intellectual, and political exports." Therefore, he argues, "we want students, whatever their individual ancestries, to be exposed to Western ideas, history, and institutions because such study transmits the kind of knowledge most potent for an understanding of the contemporary world. To do anything else would be to cheat them of the most significant benefit an education can provide, the capacity for enjoying a meaningful freedom."

I don't know about you, but as a university president who feels that he's been dragged through a sea of truisms and caricatures once too often in the past year, and who begins feeling a bit queasy whenever he hears the word "diversity," I find that a subtle and rather powerful argument—one, at any rate, that encourages further thought. And let me say first that, as an argument, it's still missing a basic point, which I will summarize with a dash of autobiography.

When I and my fellow members of Columbia's Class of 1959 confronted the challenges—above all, the enormous reading lists—of such famous freshman and sophomore courses as Humanities and Contemporary Civilization, we often found ourselves quite "turned on" and didn't get permanently discouraged even when we arrived at the first Humanities 101 class on a Friday and were told (a) to read the entire *Iliad*, all 24 books of it, over the weekend, and (b) to come to class on Monday prepared to take a quiz on it.

How was that possible after such a Parris Island experience? It was because so many of us came from backgrounds we could summarize in a few words: New York, immigrant, upwardly mobile. Whether our parents or grandparents or great-grandparents had arrived from Sicily or Ireland, Russia or Poland, Calabria or Greece—whether their religious roots were Catholic or Jewish—they came out of cultures that were regarded as marginal. They shared a common sense of pain, for example, when reading the poetry and prose of T. S. Eliot, with its obvious contempt for those from other than what are now called "WASP" backgrounds.

For us to master the Western tradition, therefore, and to put it through its paces in our searching, critical, dispassionate, and relentlessly analytic term papers was to gain a symbolic victory over all that had once seemed to reject and threaten our forebears. We were also, I hasten to add, the last generation of undergraduates whose earliest acculturation preceded the Age of Television. Typically, we had been born in the late 1930s. When TV swept the land in the late '40s and early '50s, we were already approaching our teens. That meant that quite a few of us had grown up as what were even then called "heavy readers"—kids who actually read books voluntarily, often at their neighborhood public libraries, in addition to what they were required to read for school, which was typically a lot less interesting!

So we were "out people," from suspiciously non-WASP cultural backgrounds, of a kind hard to picture today. If our parents or grandparents lived in Sicily, for example, then the psychological scarring they communicated to their Columbia students had a lot to do with the fact that Italians of the North, especially those living in or near Milan, had long dismissed Sicilians as "africani," a sentiment often echoed by American prejudices of the time, whose true decline began in the 1960s.

But suppose Joe Napolitano (not his real name) of the Class of 1959 actually managed to understand Dante better than all of those snow-white Northerners? What could that be other than a great victory? And suppose Stanley Goldsmith (also a pseudonym), whose grandfather still talked of being jostled off sidewalks by passersby hissing "Zhid!" at him, actually produced some new insights into *King Lear* or *War and Peace*? Wouldn't that symbolize a rebalancing of accounts? Wouldn't that lessen the cosmic yet oh-so-personal injustice of an anti-Semitic vendetta relentlessly pursued over a period of at least a millennium and a half?

Not that we ever actually articulated such a program of sweet revenge. Indeed, the fact that it was unvoiced may have made it more powerful. But what it all added up to was that the Western tradition had a certain "hook" for us—that it elicited not just a coldly intellectual response but also an emotional response, even if what we went on to write in a term paper or an exam essay was cast in the neutral tones of modern scholarship. In the process, we acquired the skills and achieved the grades we needed to make our way in an America whose wildly booming postwar economy did turn out to have room for us.

And the question I find unanswered by the National Academy of Scholars and others on their side of the debate is this: Where is that special *hook* to come from when we are dealing with the black and brown and Hispanic minorities who will soon, taken together, form a majority of the American population?

To take a look at the true "other side," consider the words of a tweed-jacketed professor soon to join the Harvard University English Department faculty. Said Henry Louis Gates, Jr., who happens to be an African American, in a recent magazine interview:

"I read an article recently that said that one of the things that was 'acting white' for black high school kids in Washington was going to the Smithsonian. Fewer things have made me more depressed than that about the state of black America. When I drive to my house and go through the black neighborhood that's between two white neighborhoods, I don't see black kids packing books at 5 o'clock. They have a basketball, and they're going down to the courts. We have to change the erroneous assumption that you have a better chance of being Magic Johnson than you do of being a brain surgeon. There are more black lawyers than black professional athletes."

That touches my heart. It tells me that, where minority undergraduates are concerned, "getting through" is our greatest challenge and will require, at the very least, some serious compromises by those in tune with NAS's pedagogical philosophy, even in the sophisticated version presented by Stephen Balch. Because if we don't "get through," and soon, what can we expect our world of higher education to look and feel like as we move toward the year 2000? Indeed, what will our whole country look like and feel like, given the extent to which businesses and industries here, unlike those in Japan and western Germany, depend on our academic system to do their skills training and personnel screening for them?

What form the compromises might take is a tough question. Perhaps we could start with what Columbia's humanities program only got to in its second year: art and music. Might we use the superb Benin bronzes of West Africa, for example, to "bait the hook" for African American students? Or, for the white student "radical" from a "good suburban high school" who's in the process of rejecting every tenet of his or her acculturation, might we begin with a comparison of the early Buddhist art of the Greek-influenced "Gandharan" culture of north-western India with the art produced by the great Zen painters of medieval Japan? Or, for the undergraduate who believes that jazz and life are synonyms, might we compare, say, improvisatory music from the West with that of Africa and India (which would line up perfor-mances on piano, drums, and sitar)?

But all that sounds so custom tailored. In a decade when cutbacks and personnel reductions are the order of the day, how could we plan and administer such innovative programs without sending academic budgets through the ceiling?

I don't have the answers to such questions—nor, I suspect, does any-one else. And that's the point. Once we are able to work our way past the media's oversimplifications, with what I've called their cardboard-cutout caricatures eternally going at each other like Punch and Judy, the really interesting dialogues can begin.

1 9 9 2

PRODUCTIVITY
AND THE ACADEMIC "BUSINESS"

ADAPTED FROM AN ARTICLE IN *PRODUCTIVITY AND HIGHER
EDUCATION: IMPROVING THE EFFECTIVENESS OF FACULTY, FACILITIES,
AND FINANCIAL RESOURCES* (PETERSON'S GUIDES, 1992)

Never has productivity in higher education been more important than it is today. Virtually every American college and university is struggling to bring in more revenue without adding unnecessary expenditures. And it is this concern for revenue, as much as any "pure" concern for undergraduate education, that has been driving the new calls for a better balance between teaching and research in our academic institutions.

Increasingly, university administrators have had to face the fact that while undergraduate tuition provides a vital portion of the money they spend on personnel and facilities, undergraduates do not always directly benefit from those expenditures. So while many institutions continue to be possessed by a "faculty-researcher star syndrome," responsible academic leaders are paying closer attention to how institutional funds are being distributed, and particularly to how the allocations affect undergraduate opportunities.

This emphasis on the "business" side of the equation tends to provoke furious resentment in the hearts of most professors and many administrators. I suspect that such people will not be pleased by the following parable (whose fictional characters should not be confused with any actual human beings, living or dead). But to me, it's a story worth thinking about.

The Parable

Once I decided to compose these words, I asked my university's physics department and engineering school to create a time-travel machine for me. They came through in record time and, with the help of our law school, the gadget was quickly patented. Our business school was soon negotiating the machine's sale to a Japanese company that promised to build its primary plant on our new campus in Northern Virginia.

It was just a few weeks before beginning the first draft that I clambered into this remarkable machine, not without some trepidation, and made my voyage back to 1959, when I was a senior at the undergraduate men's college of Columbia University.

It was as if I had never left. Indeed, I kept expecting to run into myself, rushing across the quad on the way to class. Instead, I literally bumped into the university president, who was crossing the campus at his usual stately pace, homburg firmly in place, herringbone tweed impeccably fitted, gray mustache neatly trimmed.

"I beg your pardon, Mr. President," I said, "but you happen to be exactly the person I'm looking for. Could we please sit down on this bench here and talk a moment? I need to ask you an important question."

Although he looked skeptical, he did agree to join me on the bench, whereupon I began the following disquisition:

"Mr. President, I know this will seem a bit unbelievable, but you've probably noticed by now that I bear an eerie middle-aged resemblance to one of the seniors currently attending the college—an energetic and rather involved young man named Stephen Joel Trachtenberg. I assure you, though, that I am not his father or his uncle. I am *he himself*. And I've come here all the way from the early 1990s—when I, too, am a university president—to ask you how you feel about the subject of productivity and the academic business."

When he heard those words, the president acquired an expression of complete disbelief.

"Young man," he began—in those days you were considered a young man, probably quite rash and feckless, until you were on the verge of 60—"I congratulate you on your vivid imagination, as well as your remarkable resemblance to the student you mentioned. Next time, however, make certain that you don't venture too far from the realm of plausibility. Serious academic study will never be a *business*, as you so laughably suggest. And as for *productivity*, if I heard you correctly, I suppose that has something to do with *factories* that make *things*, like automobiles and refrigerators, and therefore could not be applied to the purposes and ideals of our universities as those institutions have grown and developed for nearly 1,000 years."

Then, without awaiting further comment from me, he rose and marched off toward the library. Meanwhile, my beeper began summoning me for the return trip to my own time. I pushed through the gaggle of students and security guards surrounding my time machine, which was parked illegally on the campus, and quickly made my way back to the future—or, rather, to the present. But when I reached my own university in Washington, I was immediately confronted by an unofficial delegation of five colleagues who announced that they had urgent business with me.

"I'm sorry to inform you, sir," said the first, "that we are very upset by your plans to submit an article for publication on the subject of productivity and the academic business. Frankly, we regard the subject as the absolute nadir of some of the worst trends in the academic world of the past 10 years. We are profoundly disturbed that the president of our university is making such a spectacle of himself!"

"Spectacle?" I asked. "Is it a spectacle to join a group of distinguished authors to explore the notion that even not-for-profit institutions require actual money to pay for salaries and fringe benefits—not to mention building maintenance, landscaping, library acquisitions, student services, admissions work, financial aid programs, laboratory supplies, and data processing equipment?"

"You don't understand," said Colleague No. 2 with a faint smile. "That's what the *administration* is there for. It's *your* function to raise the money, and it's the role of faculty governance to make the decisions on how it ought to be spent. We're the ones on the academic front lines. We're the ones who understand, better than anyone else possibly can, the needs posed by our professional commitments to our students. For you to refer to productivity and the academic business . . . well, that implies quite a different kind of metaphor, one drawn from the *corporate* sector of the economy, where altogether different rules apply."

"Exactly right, Mr. President" agreed Colleague No. 3. "And we are inclined to regard talk of productivity and business as a counterrevolution against the hard-won rights and privileges of the American professoriate. I suspect that you'd prefer the position of a traditional boss, seeking to extract 'productivity' from the assembly line."

"Absolutely right!" exclaimed Colleague No. 4. "All of us know that where higher education is concerned, definitions of productivity are entirely subjective except by the grossest of financial measures. Do you mean teaching productivity in terms of hours spent in the classroom or number of students taught? Do you mean teaching productivity in terms of quality—and if so, quality defined by whom? Or do you mean teaching productivity in terms of long-term benefits received by students? And how would you go about measuring that, when it's a fact that individuals benefit from higher education in different ways at different points in their lives, all the way through to their senior-citizen years?

"Or perhaps you mean research productivity," No. 4 continued. "But how would you measure that? It took me 12 years to complete my absolutely definitive monograph on an obscure but highly influential poet of the 16th century. And in all those years I published not a single article or book review. Should I be considered less productive than someone from another discipline who, in the same length of time, published 20 articles or three books? And if by any chance you mean *financial* productivity—the ability of professors to attract business, as you call it, and to maximize the payoff on the hours they invest in the classroom or laboratory—how could such a system favor anyone who isn't a wildly popular teacher with huge lecture classes or a super researcher pulling in massive government funds or foundation grants?"

I cleared my throat.

"My friends," said I, "aren't you overreacting to what is, after all, just the working title of a modest chapter in a book? Most of it, in fact, won't even address academic matters but will be concerned with things like financial management, intellectual property, facilities management, and. . . ."

"Hogwash!" exclaimed Colleague No. 5, unable to contain herself. "You aren't dealing with illiterates, you know. You're dealing with Ph.D.'s who can spot the thin edge of a wedge when they see it. Don't think we've missed the news that British universities are terminating professors for financial reasons. They can't attract enough students to cover their own paychecks and fringe benefits—meaning, presumably, that they're insufficiently *productive*. They've already let a professor of philosophy go. Next to be deemed unprofitable—thrown out on their ears at the age of 40 or 50—will be those working on the 'wrong' languages or literatures, the ones working in anthropology rather than computer science, and, of course, the ones working in pure science rather than business or applied technology.

"By contributing to a book like this, Mr. President, you are certain to help create a climate for similar moves in this country!" No. 5 concluded.

And there we stood, my colleagues and I, looking at one another across a gap as wide as the Grand Canyon.

"Colleagues," I said in a slightly quivering voice, "forgive me for getting personal, but do you have any idea how hard we have to run in order to stay, financially, in the same place? At the beginning of this year our costs for major medical insurance at this university went up 94 percent. The work we're doing to attract better students has required massive increases in our scholarship program. And at a time when the most elite universities and colleges have moved well over the

$20,000 mark for a single year's tuition, it's no surprise that people are talking—even complaining—about academic productivity."

There followed about 30 seconds of silence, broken finally by Colleague No. 3.

"You're trying to panic us," he snapped, "and it's not going to work. Your methodology is entirely unsound. I haven't heard a single relevant fact or piece of solidly grounded data in what you've been saying since this discussion began. How can you possibly go through with this article?"

"Well," I replied, "I am committed to this. But having reflected on your concerns about these matters, I will think about adding a subtitle—perhaps something like this: *The Single Most Urgent and Possibly Insoluble Problem Confronting Higher Education in a Period of Escalating Costs, Escalating Tuition, and Growing Disenchantment Among Average Americans, Corporate Leaders, and Legislators with the Academic Enterprise As It Is Presently Defined and Conducted in the United States.*

"It does give the essay a distinctly more academic ring, doesn't it?" I remarked as I turned to the technicians and ordered them to destroy the time-travel machine as quickly as possible.

Then I left the group and headed straight for my office to tell our business dean that the machine was no longer for sale. The last thing I wanted to inflict on higher education was evidence that the vision of academic life shared by most academicians had scarcely changed since the late 1950s . . . even as the world around us continues to change a very great deal indeed!

The Reality

The day is long past when any university's faculty members, administrators, or staff can take its elegant seals, ceremonies, maces, and robes as a kind of divine guarantee that the payroll will always be met and life will always remain stable. Even the strongest Fortune 500 companies, which have capitalization sufficient to carry them through several very lean years, are currently looking at their budgets—right down to the most trivial but collectively huge expenditures—with eagle eyes and trembling hearts.

This is not a parable. The fiscal future of the entire United States is currently in question. Contrary prophecies and scenarios regarding that future long ago leaped from the pages of major business journals and newspaper and news-magazine business sections, into the daily parlance of the American people. In a world of this kind, it must be clearly understood that independent institutions of higher education are "independent" only insofar as they cannot, at present, be *directly* told what to do by government agencies.

But as long as independent schools exist by the acts of sufferance known as governmental charters, even that could change if our national and international economic situation becomes sufficiently serious. It behooves us all to think and act accordingly. Every person on a university's payroll, as well as alumni and friends, must introduce a strong component of responsible fiscal thinking into their efforts on behalf of that university.

And please note that I have not once used the word *productivity* in this conclusion. What's the sense in bringing up such a volatile word when the real need it represents is having a hard enough time on its own?

SHORT TAKES II

THE GOALS OF HIGHER EDUCATION

W e should not minimize the significance of The George Washington University's Baptist roots, as well as the fact that its earliest presidents came from such strongly religious backgrounds.

The major world religions—including Judaism, Christianity, and Islam—have always put teaching alongside revelation at the core of their value systems. What those early administrators and their faculty colleagues sought to achieve was a university that would serve the national need—but would do so guided by the North Star of ethical and humane behavior.

From the very start they rejected the notion of making this a sectarian institution. From the very start they sought to place it at the service of a nation committed to the cause of humanity—a nation that they prayed would pursue self-interest up to a certain point, but not to the point at which self-interest was its only pursuit. From the start, therefore, they saw the function of deeply committed teaching as one that would distinguish this university, functioning in the most influential of all American cities.

At the national level, each industrialized country is having to struggle toward a new balance between the process of industrial development and the preservation of what industrial development was originally meant to serve, namely the quality of our individual and collective lives. Gone is the day when those concerned with the quality of life were regarded as enemies of those seeking to give us more and better products with which to improve life. With something close to culture shock, we are beginning to realize that, like fish in a pond, we are all in this together.

Meanwhile, within higher education, the long reign of disciplinary separation and specialization is giving way to a search, however inchoate, for common ground linking technological achievement with humanistic concern, objectivity with ethics, analysis with synthesis, ends with means.

—Remarks at the Inauguration of Stephen Joel Trachtenberg
as 15th President of The George Washington University, April 16, 1989

Universities and colleges deal in information. That is how they earn their money. In an information age as dynamic as the one we now inhabit, either they will learn to be dynamic themselves or they will be replaced—and the contenders for the privilege of educating postsecondary students are already lining up. They are collectively known as America's corporate sector, and the money they spend educating their employees is approaching $100 billion a year. It could be increased even more if the federal government provides tax credits, and could easily be extended to encompass potential employees.

—Remarks at the "Outlook 2010" Conference,
Fairfax County Public Schools, McLean, Va., April 18, 1990

Universities like George Washington, I would argue, are the only true multinational melting pots on earth. They are places where students from around the world—potentially even from warring nations—gather in the same classrooms to hear the same professors give the same lectures. They are places where these same students have the opportunity to interact, to share insights, experiences, and opinions about issues of the day. And they are places, we hope, where citizens of different countries and cultures come to understand and enlighten others.

International graduates of these universities are destined to return to their countries with newfound knowledge and understanding—and not just within their particular courses of study. They are destined to know more about the United States and other countries and to have personal knowledge of, and friendships with, individuals from around the world. On returning to their countries, they are destined to share this knowledge with friends, families, and colleagues at work.

By fostering such experiences—such global transfers of knowledge and understanding—I feel we can do no wrong. It can only be healthy for the nations of the world to have a greater knowledge within their borders of what lies beyond them. The alternative, ignorance, is perhaps the most significant threat we face in the quest for peace and global cooperation.

If our governments were to spend on defense what we all currently spend on education, and on education what we now lay out for defense, our armed forces and our educational systems would both improve. And both would be significantly more responsive to the realities of the modern world.

—Remarks at Moscow State University, Moscow, May 1991

As universities and colleges learn to share their resources, research costs will come down. Teaching, meanwhile, has achieved a cachet that would have seemed most unlikely even two or three years ago. Indeed, major research universities like Stanford are now in the forefront of institutions promising, at long last, to reward excellent teaching as they have rewarded, until recently, relatively mediocre research.

And the "new day a-dawning" will come as good news not only to undergraduates and their families, but also to the 80 percent or so of American faculty members who regularly confide in nationwide polls that their research and publishing has a lot more to do with their desire for advancement than a quest for truth.

Indeed, what we now need to keep in mind is that good teaching is always based on the type of instructorial energy and commitment that make a personal "research program" almost mandatory. And while good research *can* be conducted by those indifferent or hostile toward the "waste of time" involved in teaching, it is a great deal more common for the enthusiasm and commitment of a well-motivated researcher to "overflow." The beneficiaries of this process may be research assistants or undergraduates—but beneficiaries there will be.

—"The Difficult Quest for Balance in American Higher Education,"
in The World & I, The Washington Times Corporation, December 1991

In the 1980s, the world of higher education saw verbal inflation—that's neatly structured hot air—proceed at a rate that could have filled all the floats in New York's Thanksgiving Day Parade. What used to be called "normal schools" became colleges, colleges became universities, programs became departments, lecturers became professors, and scholarly sub-specializations declared themselves to be world-class institutes that of course needed their own buildings, clerical staff, computers, and logos.

—Remarks to the National Council for Resource Development,
Washington, D.C., December 10, 1991

The American inability to deal with the education of our children at the elementary and secondary levels has a kind of malign complement in the American tendency to treat higher education in magical or fetishistic terms—as a place onto which to project all kinds of contradictory wishes, hopes, and demands.

These projections help to account for a lot of the demoralization in our universities and four-year colleges. Our universities are now suffering from a sense of *conflicted mission*. Unlike most professionals in our society—unlike physicians, lawyers, and engineers, for example—those who now work under the title of *professor* are very often deeply uncertain as to what *exactly* they ought to be doing.

Should our institutions of higher education be emphasizing research missions and goals of demonstrated importance—missions that may prove critical to the innovative power of the American economy, and therefore to America's position in the international economy? Or do the institutions need to focus on what amounts to mass remedial education, as they seek to compensate for the failures of our nation's public schools?

—Remarks at the Mitre Corporation's "Distinguished Lecture Series,"
Bedford, Mass., February 25, 1992

Colleges and universities have been created—and have created themselves—in order to embody a tradition of self-scrutiny. If it gets transmitted, and if our graduates apply it to their own lives and adult functions, then there is hope for the future of American society and its role in our ever-more-interdependent world. If it *doesn't* get transmitted, and if graduates go on to lives driven by short-term "input" and an absence of rigorous reasoning, then the American decline that so many of us fear is upon us will in fact turn out to be not the wave but the trough of our collective future.

—Remarks at the 27th Annual Conference, Society for College and University Planning, Minneapolis, Minn., August 3, 1992

There are some minuses as higher education seeks to become more responsive to society's needs. The system risks losing a good deal of what used to be considered its relaxing charm—all of the images once associated with the "Halls of Ivy." We also risk losing the kinds of faculty members who might once have meditated for 20 years before producing a massive and definitive book. Students who want to explore freely—to do some intellectual wandering—may find everybody around them too intent on specialties, jobs, and careers. *Serendipity*, once considered an academic virtue, may fall victim to *productivity*. Those are risks we need to guard against, of course. But they're inevitable risks, and we will inevitably fall prey to at least some of them in the new era of our bitterly competitive international economy.

In the future, many of our colleges and universities are going to have to become more specialized. For universities, that's a particular challenge—because it means that universal functioning is no longer possible for them. Difficult choices have to be made and are *being* made. That's why even major universities have started to phase out entire departments, schools, and divisions—especially those whose enrollments are low and whose intellectual or practical value is dubious. That's why public universities with multiple campuses have begun to insist that duplicate functions be minimized—and that a student is often perfectly capable of traveling from Campus A to Campus B to obtain a particular kind of instruction. And that's why more and more colleges and universities, including some private ones, are exploring cooperative efforts, such as sharing expensive equipment.

—Remarks at the D.C. Jewish Community Center's John R. Risher Public Affairs Forum, Washington, D.C., May 6, 1993

The growing controversy over remedial education and the community colleges is understandable. The President argues that we need to expand access to higher education, and that is important. Also, community colleges are appropriate for many students. But what transpires in those institutions cannot be a waste of time and money. At an absolute minimum, someone coming out of a community college ought to be able to read a manual, follow directions, communicate, do quantitative stuff, and use a computer.

—Interview at The George Washington University, February 2, 1998

It's amusing sometimes to think that—in an environment in which academic people talk so much about human values—we are so much like the rest of the world, which is perhaps less sanctimonious about it. It turns out that in the university, selfish motives and other terribly human characteristics are every bit as widespread as they are in labor unions, in management groups, in organizations for profit and not for profit. Politics and personality do play out in the deliberations of the institution—and we are less pure and less good at living the life we advocate than arguably we should be.

As more and more people have a university experience, and are therefore less in awe of universities and less daunted by scholars, we are being called to account with more regularity. The people can't be buffaloed, because they're not ignorant. I mean, we have created our own critics by educating them. This means that we're going to have to live up to a higher standard.

—Interview at The George Washington University, February 2, 1998

1 9 9 3

WHY IT MATTERS
HOW WE CUT THE CAKE

GRADUATION SPEECH AT THE SIDWELL FRIENDS SCHOOL,
WASHINGTON, D.C., JUNE 11, 1993

My daytime job, of course, is being president of The George Washington University. But it is when I go home at night that I really start to work.

That is because at home I am a *paterfamilias*; I am husband and father. And as the father of two sons, I spend a great deal of time thinking about equity. That's how you can tell I am the father: *I* think about equity. My *sons*, especially when they were younger, have called the same idea "fairness." Such semantic differences between the generations may seem amusing, but the meaning inside the words is no laughing matter—and, believe me, it never was.

If my wife and I brought the boys gifts, they had to be exactly the same. Even a different color could set off a dispute between Adam and Ben. For a father concerned about equity, this cut to the heart of the job. And speaking of cutting, consider what happened when it came time to cut a cake for dessert. One son could cut the cake, but then son No. 2 got the first lick of the cake knife . . . *this* time. Next time, I would have to remember who got first cut and first lick *last* time. And then, you know, not all licks are the same. Did the cake in question this time have a very thick, buttery, creamy icing that stuck more plentifully to the knife than the thinner chocolate icing of the previous cake? Does the first lick of the knife mean *both* sides of the blade? Was it the same knife—or was the knife we used last time larger?

I hasten to add that the particular intellectual constructs of equity or the practical applications of fairness I employed to solve the problem of cutting the cake were of no use at all when the question was who got what from the mixing bowl used for cookie dough, or who went down the slide in the playground first, or who got to answer the phone.

My sons are teenagers now. Cutting the cake or having identical blue water pistols are not problems anymore. But fairness still is—even if, as young men with their own views of the world, they are beginning to think and talk about it as equity. Even if their thoughts about equity are turning to what philosophers call "distributive justice." And even if they are genuinely concerned about how equity applies to others, not only themselves.

From this I conclude that my sons were paying more attention than their mother and father ever suspected. I also conclude that cutting the cake is a problem that never goes away. It's just that the cake doesn't look like a cake. It tends to look like the job market, or access to opportunity, or health care, or getting into the college of your choice, or something else—but always something. It looks like life.

I am thrilled that my sons are beginning to think in these terms—no more so than all your parents and relatives are thrilled with all of your growth and accomplishments, which we are celebrating today. But all this presents me right now with a bit of a problem—two problems, actually, and you could call both of them "telling the truth."

First, as you know, graduation speakers are supposed to talk about a commencement, not a graduation. As if "graduation" (which comes from the Latin *gradus*, meaning "step") is just too pale a word next to "commencement," which, of course, means "beginning." But if what I have been telling you about my own sons is true, and if the stories all your parents could tell on similar subjects are also true, then today is hardly the beginning of anything for you. In fact, it's the end of high school.

So if I were to tell you that today you are commencing, you might ask, "What? What am I commencing *today*?" And what am I supposed to say? "Your life?" If I say that, you'll find a way of reminding me—maybe even politely—that you've been alive for 17 or 18 years, and you will ask, "So what was I doing up to now? Wasn't I learning to cut the cake? You mean going to Sidwell and dealing with my hormones and getting a driver's license weren't living?"

Or maybe a nice young man—who happens to be one of you, graduating today—would tell me a little story about life and living. A couple of months ago, he thought it was time to line something up for his senior project. So he got on the phone and called an appropriately virtuous and utterly blameless social service agency. He introduced himself and said, "I have to do some community service." Without a moment's hesitation, the voice at the other end of the phone asked him, "Who's your probation officer?"

This nice young man from Sidwell Friends, this young man who was not yet 18 years old, learned that all of us are living in a society in which "community service" is a synonym for the soft alternative to doing hard time. It is *not*, in the minds of most people, our personal and voluntary effort to bring some measure of equity to an inequitable world. It's regarded not as the hard work of justice, but as the easy way out of the criminal justice system. I'm more than three times his age, and I hadn't begun to learn that. Or, you could say, I learned that from *his* life. And you all have your stories, too. So much for beginnings today.

That's just the first problem. If I abandon the routine flights of fancy on the theme of commencement and decide, along with you, I hope, to be contented with the notion of graduation as "step taking," then I face the second problem of the speaker who wants to be truthful.

The standard and official version of the step-taking graduation speech tells you to "Step out! Pick up the torch! Make the world better than the one your parents and I gave you! You may take three giant steps! Go forth! Be strong!"

Of course, nearly all of you are going forth now, but mostly to a summer vacation or a job and then to college. You will not be governing the nation, ending inequity, or distributing world peace where it's needed most. But I'm very glad that you're going to college, which will be very different from Sidwell Friends. It's my life's work to make sure that it's different, but it's not your *life*. It's another step—and God willing, it will end with another step-taking ceremony, another graduation.

The step of going to college may be your defining moment. I know it was for me—or, at least, for part of my life. As an undergraduate at Columbia, I began asking myself, What am I really good at? The answer was, student government. That led to the question: So how do you make a living out of this? The first part of the answer was simple: Remain a student as long as you possibly can, and hope for a combination of understanding parents and generous grants. There followed a series of more difficult questions and answers that helped me shape my working life.

But college may *not* be the defining moment for you. And remember, in my case, this was just one step (a good step) leading to my day job, which is how I earn my living. But it was not my "life." And it was not much different from the step my sons have already taken. No longer do they argue about cutting the cake. But that is not to say that there are no longer any grounds for argument or causes left for parental anxiety in our household. Adam and Ben have moved on to other agendas, and their mother and father are following in their wake.

So if what you are doing here today is not a beginning—if it's only one of many steps in your lives—then why are we gathered here? It is a rite of passage. And for good reason. Something has been happening to all of you during the last few years of your lives, and we need a ritual to mark it. This helps you see what might otherwise remain invisible. All cultures do this with—or perhaps *to*—their young. Some go in for bloodletting and tattooing at the moment of passage. Others require different clothing or new haircuts, or carrying an emblem of adulthood, perhaps a weapon. We don't do that. We give you a piece of paper suitable for framing. And unless you are a bit odd and hang your diploma around your neck, it won't show when you walk down the street. No one will be able to tell that you are now a full member of the clan or a certified defender of the faith or just old enough to come in out of the rain without being told. Our rites of passage mark something you can't see—something I'll call the power to do well and good.

You have just finished up at the finest school in Washington. If your teachers have done their job and you have done yours, then you have learned some useful and good things. Perhaps the best way to put it— and I regret to say that these apt words were first spoken by someone else—is that you have begun the lifelong process of "making the acquaintance of your own mind."

That, it seems to me, is something worth a ritual—with a pretty good party to follow. It means that you are on your way to puzzling out how to cut the many cakes that will be coming your way. It means that you possess both the power and the knowledge to choose to do good things—and to do them well—or to do otherwise. This, too, is no laughing matter, and it's something Mr. Vogel would want you to understand.

When I was in seventh grade, all the boys took what we used to call "shop." While the girls learned to sew and cook English muffin pizzas, the boys learned to distinguish a brad from a nail, male plugs from female, and other cultural artifacts presumed to be indispensable to a young man. I will not dwell on the notion that such distinctions based on gender are now widely regarded as the wrong way to cut the cake.

Our shop teacher was Mr. Vogel, a lovely and humane person, an artisan and a teacher, who loved sharing his craft with his students. I was a source of despair to Mr. Vogel because my bookends ended too soon or too late, my tie racks were wracked or untied, and my lamps would not light.

Nevertheless, I learned three useful and good things in Mr. Vogel's shop class. First, I learned to respect a skilled worker. Second, I learned to avoid hammer, saw, and, most especially, a vice—of all kinds. And third, I learned what Mr. Vogel meant when I went to him with my current project in pieces, saying, "Look, Mr. Vogel, it broke."

Mr. Vogel would say, "Trachtenberg, it didn't break. You broke it."

Mr. Vogel was right. The cake doesn't cut itself inequitably; *we* cut it. But if now you can break things or make the wrong cut, you have also arrived at a time in your life when you know how to fix things and cut straight and fairly.

This is the power you have now, and it is a very good reason to be here today. We're celebrating your accomplishments and your acquisition of intellectual tools. But it's more significant, I think, that we're celebrating the future successes of prosperity and equity that you have the power to make for yourselves and for others in your communities. Not just in your day jobs, but in your real work—in your lives.

THE IMPORTANCE
OF ANCIENT HISTORY

REMARKS AT THE COLUMBIA UNIVERSITY CONVOCATION,
NEW YORK CITY, AUGUST 31, 1993

Thirty-eight years ago, when the world was young, I sat where you are sitting now—together with the other members of the Class of 1959—and listened to Dean Nicholas McKnight as he tried to electrify us with the importance of our Columbia education. And when he pointed his forefinger in our general direction, and declared that sitting among us there might very well be a future winner of the Nobel Prize, I was personally electrified. Would that brilliant and world-famous individual turn out to be *me*?

So as I made my way from Columbia College through the various stages of my career, I actually experienced mad, immodest moments when McKnight's words came crowding inadvertently back into my mind. I'd stand there in front of the bathroom mirror, making faces at myself, with shaving cream on my cheeks, and I'd ask myself: "Does what I'm doing with my life right now make it more or less likely that the King of Sweden will one day be draping the Nobel Prize around my neck and passing along to me a very generous check?"

And then it happened: To my delight, a fellow member of the Class of '59, Professor Roald Hoffmann, now of Cornell University, won the Nobel Prize for Chemistry. Roald is a modern-style chemist and a poet. He does his work not in a laboratory with test tubes and beakers and Bunsen burners, but in an office—with computers. And when the announcement came about his Nobel Prize, I sent him a letter of rejoicing, just so he'd have some idea of the weight he had lifted from my weary, unworthy shoulders. Rather than be chasing so unlikely a possibility as the Nobel Prize, I could finally settle down to the calm, placid, and dignified life of a university president—someone whose day-to-day worries focused on modest matters of institutional finance, legal actions, curricular upheaval, faculty disputations, journalistic and political denunciations, and the occasional student excesses.

But now, as I get ready to say a few words to you—words that, if they stay with you at all beyond tomorrow's lunch, hopefully won't do so in quite as compulsive a way as those that Dean McKnight spoke in 1955—I find myself filled with what one might call chronological doubt.

If this were 1965, I'd tell you what a great, contemplative place Columbia College is—and not to feel too anxious about the recent demonstrations on campus, including the riotous occupation of President Kirk's office, because the measure of a Columbia education cannot be affected by such transient historical eruptions.

And if this were 1975, I'd tell you what a great, contemplative place Columbia College is—and not to feel too anxious about runaway inflation, because the value of a Columbia education even has a material aspect. Those whose minds have been sharpened here will be able to carve a successful career for themselves, even with mortgage rates moving toward 16 percent.

If this were 1985, on the other hand, I'd tell you what a great, contemplative place Columbia College is—and not to be swept away by the excessive quest for wealth that has become the hallmark of the Reagan years. A Columbia education enables one to rise above such Niagaras of mass enthusiasm as the love of cash and the lust for expensive goodies that is animating the American *Zeitgeist*.

But this is none of those years; it is 1993—a time of fingernail-chomping worry about jobs and careers and the international economy. So the question I'm asking myself runs as follows: "Once I get through telling them what a great, contemplative place Columbia College is, and how much I enjoyed my four years here on *Spectator* and Student Board, and how later my Columbia education helped me at every point in my own personal and professional life, then what else can I say to them at a time as frequently scary and dismaying as the present?"

It's fair to note, without becoming sentimental, that what happens between today and commencement is likely to have an impact on your development. The campus, the teachers, and the city all create a special experience that forms Columbia men and women. And you can always tell Columbia men and women—though you can't tell them much.

A few words of counsel: What you need to be during your years as a Columbia student, and your subsequent years as a Columbia graduate, is ruthless, suspicious, and utterly devoid of compromise.

Be ruthless with yourself. Just because one of your instructors likes the work you've done is no reason to be content. Maybe he or she was just having a good day, and it carried over into the grading. Keep your personal, intellectual, and ethical standards even higher than those of your teachers and bosses, and you can't go wrong. Be morbidly suspicious of everything you're told—particularly at events like this and by people like me, who may reflect too uncritically on the Columbia they knew as undergraduates—and of everything you read. In a world that plays as fast and loose with evidence as the one we're living in, a world in which seeing is not believing, Columbia's traditional emphasis on primary as opposed to secondary sources has special importance.

Finally, I suggest that you be utterly devoid of compromise—at least where intellectual matters are concerned. Don't let the historical phenomenon called fanaticism give dedication a bad name. Never change your mind unless someone gives you an excellent reason for doing so. Be critical and ask hard questions that go right to the core, even if that core has been venerated by generations of Columbia students.

But as you practice this high degree of ruthlessness, suspiciousness, and utter refusal to compromise, do not forget the virtue known as compassion. And just to make sure you don't forget it, I'm going to exercise it in front of your very eyes.

Seated in your midst is a brand new Columbia freshman whose last name is the same as my own and whose first name is Adam. He's been listening to me for more than 18 years now—at the breakfast table, over lunch, at dinnertime, and under other circumstances as well. Finally he gets away from home. Finally he comes all the way to New York and to Morningside Heights. And what should he hear once he gets here but that old familiar voice. I feel flooded with compassion for Adam when I think of it. I hope you do, too.

I know that with your contribution, Columbia College will move forward from strength to strength—remaining a place of joy, a place where the standard of excellence is tempered by civility, decency, and humanity. I'll conclude these remarks by saying that I've looked at every one of you in the course of making them, and that all of you look like Nobel Prize winners to me!

1994

THE DEATH AND REBIRTH
OF EMPATHY

ARTICLE IN *TRUSTEESHIP* (ASSOCIATION OF GOVERNING BOARDS
OF UNIVERSITIES AND COLLEGES), SEPTEMBER/OCTOBER 1994

Pick up your daily newspaper and you are likely to find a front-page story along the following lines: At age 53, after 20 years of highly competent service in the engineering department of a large corporation, your neighbor-right-down-the-block has been fired. His company, like so many others, is "downsizing" for the third or fourth time since 1990. He has been unable to find another job above the fast-food level ($5.75 an hour, without benefits) and has had to turn to the municipality for assistance—otherwise known as welfare—because his wife is dying of cancer. He doubts that even the current economic upturn will change his situation "because once you're in your 50s they stop taking you seriously as a job candidate. They're looking for appli-cants in their 20s. And just try proving it in a court of law."

The article portrays your neighbor as representative of a whole class of people in your town, in our country, and in today's world. "In a bru-tally competitive economy," the reporter declares as the story contin-ues onto the business page, "those who can be cut from the payroll will be cut. And there are too many of them for us to pay real attention anymore—worried as we all are about our own situations. With their college diplomas and graduate degrees and middle-management jobs, they seemed to be doing everything exactly right. And now that they have reached their years of maturity, they find themselves vocationally and sometimes physically homeless."

Has anyone ventured an estimate of what this new world of ours, in which empathy has become unfashionable, is doing to the spirit of higher education? The postwar expansion of America's colleges and universities coincided, after all, with a now-memorable and oft-memo-rialized boom of the American economy. Indeed, Clark Kerr's "multi-versity" derived its strength and omnipresence from the fact that it was serving that economy in so many ways. And in a world with a diminishing fear (at least where Americans were concerned) of not being able to earn a living—a world, moreover, just beginning to confront the realities and tactile horrors of World War II—the flowering of prewar humanities and "great books" courses into a mass curriculum also represented a great flowering of a process that soon received an official title: *empathy*.

Our colleges taught literature and history, physics and sociology, but above all they taught compassion. "Break out of the potential parochial envelope of your self-concern," they urged their students via many different words and attitudes and postures. "Learn to contemplate how the human race has dealt with human feeling, and then watch your own life blossom."

In the paradoxical 1960s, when student activists abruptly turned their empathic fervor toward the American underclass and denounced the humanistic curricula of their colleges as typical examples of Western elitism, they could still be seen as products—indeed, successful products—of their education. Then came the oil embargo of 1973, the deadly inflation of the Carter years, the arrival of Ronald Reagan, and the onset of an age in which East Asia rather than America provides economists with their most highly prized parables. Not the United States alone but the whole world began an awesome revolution, in the course of which compassion was redefined as a brake on enhanced productivity.

On American streets, the homeless proliferated. The problem with panhandlers of various kinds became the problem of controlling them. As a new wave of social Darwinism rampaged through the global economy, young Americans, with varying degrees of anxiety and anger, confronted the tyranny of part-time jobs, any three of which still didn't provide an income on which they could comfortably live.

Earlier this year, the *Boston Globe* quoted a Japanese social worker based in the Sanya district of Tokyo—once a synonym for full employment—as saying: "Before, the objective was to find jobs for people. Now there are not so many people who can be saved in that way. The shift is toward welfare. Some of these people can never get jobs." People who came to Sanya looking for day labor "now are looking for a place to stay, something to eat. They can't get work and haven't any money. People who had been surviving can't anymore. There are no jobs."

The article went on to quote the minister of a Japanese church as saying that "most of the people feel contempt for the jobless. However, I think the people's attitude has been changing a little. Since the recession, people start to think that might happen to them tomorrow."

As those words suggest, fear—of unemployment, downward mobility, and a loss of status and self-esteem—can bring empathy of a sort in its train. "There but for the grace of God go I" implies, at the very least, a certain kinship of catastrophe, one that may lead those still blessed with employment to alter their behavior. And such is the case for those who base their salaries on educating and preparing America's young people for economic survival.

Not too long ago, "vocationalism" was a dirty word in the context of the liberal arts. In an age of almost full employment, we delegated concern with employability to school administrators, special vocational counselors, and community colleges. The actual quest for a paying job was to be handled by the student, with a little help from professional friends.

But at the time, jobs were everywhere. Adolescents of the 1950s who were inclined toward literature and the arts discovered that the world had made a place for them and they could earn their living through empathy. They could become college professors. They could even become college professors of creative writing or painting. Such were the miracles of an Americanized economy.

Things are different now. Even those who have added M.B.A.'s to their undergraduate degrees face a profoundly uncertain job market. Colleges and universities can attribute their continuing good enrollments to the fact that men and women who receive degrees have far greater earning power than those who only manage to graduate from high school. (Indeed, the gap has been widening in recent years.) But like their students and potential students, those on college and university payrolls are also learning to "run scared."

As the downward pressure on employment has become a global concern, the U.S. Department of Education has begun to suggest that we may need to pay attention to the actual vocational outcomes of college education. Meanwhile, the Clinton administration has continued to show an interest in apprenticeship systems as possible substitutes for postsecondary schooling. The view is that, especially in light of technological advances, expanding global markets create more employment opportunities than they close off—and that people often can acquire the necessary skills through two-year colleges and on-the-job training.

For students in four-year college programs and postgraduate programs, the message is also clear. Skill—above all, the ability to rapidly acquire new skills and knowledge—has become the employment watchword of the 1990s, often in association with new forms of information technology. Skill of this kind, after all, is presumably a feature of every small business in this country and abroad that attracts venture capital of some kind, often from the mutual funds in which Americans now compulsively invest. Skill—the ability to actually do something or invent something or service something—is increasingly being seen as the only lasting key to economic survival.

When we look at the world through our students' eyes, we cannot help but feel their fears and anxieties. When we keep in mind that they and their families are now our bosses who can "fire" us by transferring to another school, we can learn to feel some useful anxieties of our own. Consider the wave of anti-academic literature that has inundated us since the 1980s, often suggesting that it is time for America to "fire" its entire system of higher education. We are now motivated toward empathy, therefore, not only by humane sentiment but also by the most basic kind of self-interest.

This empathy with our students implies several consequences for our colleges and universities. The first is this: *If you aren't thinking in terms of competition, you aren't thinking.*

Like the practitioners of every business and profession that is still holding its collective own in the 1990s, the practitioners of higher education need to feel a hot economic breath on the backs of their necks. Lawyers who advertise, physicians who enter HMO arrangements, and engineers who know they can be replaced by a skilled person seated at a computer in Bangkok or Mexico are experiencing a change of status that would have been unimaginable 20 years ago. We find ourselves living on a planet that throbs with spiritual as well as electrical energy—and an eager adaptability, ready to provide necessary services to clients located just about anywhere.

Ten years ago, it was still a heresy of sorts to refer to college students as "customers." Now they are customers in quest of jobs and skills at a time when the latter are being redefined on a pervasively individualized basis. You no longer "settle into" employment and a career, together with millions of your peers. You are offered the privilege, rather, of racing along a barely cleared and continually changing professional pathway. The day you fail to ask yourself what your job is *right now*, and whether it can be accomplished in some utterly new and more cost-effective manner, is the day you find yourself unemployed.

Much the same goes for colleges and universities. In the world we inhabit, our institutions need to look and feel like places that are trying very hard not to be replaced by some other social and educational and technological arrangement.

A second conclusion in our newly empathic condition is this: *If you aren't talking personally, you aren't being heard.*

Admissions offices participate in a familiar paradox of modern life. They must mass produce communications that have a personal, individual appeal. If the mailings and other communications sent out by XYZ University of New England successfully intersect with the exploratory ripples sent out by the Smith family of South Cudahy, Arkansas, Antonia Smith arrives at XYZ as an enrolled student.

But that is only the first step in an even more challenging process. For a period of years, Antonia and her family members must be sure that Antonia is making marked and measurable progress toward a successful life and a productive career or series of careers. Each of her instructors must see her and her family as people capable of judging, among other things, her instructors. XYZ University must convince them all—against whatever backwash of skepticism and impending disenchantment might exist—that it is honing her skills, remedying her deficits, and reciprocating her most recent tuition payments with substantial services and benefits.

Antonia and her 1,500 classmates are at XYZ in search of viable futures. Antonia and her family agonize each day over front-page stories that suggest how uncertain a future now awaits not just Antonia but her 46-year-old father and her 42-year-old mother. Their hearts beat measurably faster; their adrenaline pumps measurably harder. And those on the payroll of XYZ University have to know that—all the time. As Antonia wrestles with a paper or an exam on any subject in the curriculum, she needs to sense the ways in which that subject, and the skills it requires of those seeking to master it, connect with "the world beyond the campus." Her teachers, meanwhile, need to know what the Career Center is doing with and for their students—and when the moment has arrived to give the Career Center a buzz.

As all of this implies, not just the fear of "vocationalism" but also the old distaste for anything that smacks of *in loco parentis* are both now obsolete. The importance of the faculty member's role as a guide and adviser, a role that has steadily declined in recent years, is once again obvious. Colleges and universities need to be at least as concerned about their students' futures as are the families of those students. Those on the school payroll need to share a holographic image of each individual student and need to visualize, hanging above that image, the omnipresent question: "Would you give this student a job? If not, why not?"

Much of the criticism aimed at higher education in recent years has centered on an academic work-style perceived to be in growing contrast to the work-styles of most Americans. That is why so many state governments, as well as the U.S. Department of Education, are putting such an emphasis on the "accountability" of those who work in post-secondary education and those who teach at the primary and secondary levels. To use the popular terminology, the judgments of education at all levels are more and more "outcome oriented." The nation is judging colleges and universities by the employment their graduates actually obtain and retain. This trend intersects with a broader tide of concern among much of the American public that is expressed by such newly fashionable terms as *discipline, order,* and *moral values.*

Given how much colleges and universities—even those identified as "private" or "independent"—depend on public support, they must respond to a dramatically new and changing national perspective. The alternative is to discover, once again, just how powerful a political force resentment can be.

Those of us who have devoted our lives to higher education need to take into account the anger aroused by our seeming privileges, and especially by the badly misunderstood and often distorted institution known as tenure. We must rebuild our bridges to the American heart and declare, in effect: "We know what you are going through. We share your concern with the future of the American economy. We are doing our part by working emphatically and firmly with, and on behalf of, you and your children." And we will know we have succeeded in explaining ourselves to our benefactors, the American public and its political representatives, when our image changes—because that will mean that our realities have changed as well.

SHORT TAKES III

ADMINISTRATION
AND GOVERNANCE

We have not lived long enough to see the end of archaic modes of university governance summed up by the term "shared governance." It continues to enjoy nearly sacred status in our institutions, while the pace of faculty-senate deliberations continues to dominate the rhythms of university-wide decision making. But the fact is that we live in an increasingly tricky and dangerous world where, especially when significant amounts of money are involved, decision making must often be very, very quick if disaster is to be circumvented.

The faculty culture in higher education tends, for better or worse, to be risk averse. You don't get a Ph.D. or other major academic credential by engaging in acrobatics. You don't publish articles in refereed journals by threatening the psychological stability of the referees, or by setting their heads even mildly a-spin. On the other hand, you do conduct the fiscal affairs of a contemporary academic institution by making rapid decisions, or rapid decisions not to decide.

In relentless fashion, our universities have divided into what the late C. P. Snow called "two cultures," one of which works at decision making while the other group, which includes folks like me, makes decisions. And if the latter did otherwise, then the former would soon have reason to wonder whether a paycheck would ever again be in the works at "the usual time." That is not, in my judgment, a healthy situation.

Shared governance, in the absence of shared responsibility, will always have a certain hollow ring. At the same time, when fiscal responsibility involves the intake of vast quantities of information— much of it in numerical form—no one involved in true shared governance will find much time for research, or even an adequate amount of time to prepare for classroom teaching.

That helps explain why, when these two university cultures meet, they often start out by clashing. The slower-paced and infinitely deliberate faculty culture plays the role of the classical Tortoise. Peering out from under its shell, it accuses Brother Rabbit of behaving in a merely flighty and erratic manner. Brother Rabbit, who gets paid for avoiding all the shrapnel and machine-gun fire that currently darkens the sky, may have to summon the chairman of the board and half of its members—the more financially credentialed ones—in his own defense. They, in turn, while peering through the slits of their Fortune 500 fortresses, will generally confirm that Brother Rabbit was in the right place at the right time and out of it by the time it turned deadly.

But in such a context, "victories" are at least as counterproductive as defeats. Already sufficiently divided as they struggle to decide on their true function in today's America, universities are further divided when it comes to something as basic as the very processes of vital decision making.

—Remarks at the Mitre Corporation's "Distinguished Lecture Series," Bedford, Mass., February 25, 1992

U niversity presidents are burning out like so many moths in a room filled with lit candles.

—Remarks at the Health Policy Summer Program, The George Washington University, June 17, 1992

L ike many people who reach a certain age, I sometimes think I've seen it all. This is my 20th year as a university president and my ninth as president of The George Washington University. In all, I've been a university administrator for more than a quarter of a century. And if there's one truism I've internalized about faculty assemblies in all that time, it's that a properly conditioned university president never stands up in front of such a group without a frown and dark shadows under the eyes.

I can't do that today, however, because GW has never been in better shape. I've racked my brain for bad news to convey to you, but all I've come up with is that, no matter which traditional yardstick we employ, we're doing okay. But I do worry about one thing: taking our good fortune for granted.

Instead of remaining alert for new developments in this dangerously restless world of ours, we might mistakenly assume that we could just keep doing the same things over and over. But one day we'd find that our ferocious competitors had lured away our best students and faculty members. So let me be the first to say it: In academic life, as in most other forms of life, good fortune grants us the time and space in which to redouble our efforts. We can do no less.

—Remarks at The George Washington University's
Annual Faculty Assembly, November 1, 1996

∼

THE ROLE OF STUDENTS

Though the future of student relations will depend on the wisdom, goodwill, sense of justice, and empathic capabilities of faculty members and administrators, it will depend to an equal and sometimes even greater extent on the degree to which students can manifest these same qualities.

—"The Difficult Quest for Balance in American
Higher Education," in The World & I,
The Washington Times Corporation, December 1991

By the 1970s, those in quest of higher education changed from *petitioners* pleading for admission to *customers* inquiring after the true value of the services they *might* go on to purchase. Like all smart customers, they were suspicious. They looked at your declarations of principle with alert and skeptical eyes. And as a university president, I ceaselessly preached to my colleagues and staff what attitudinal changes they had to carry out in order to deal with these new kinds of students and their new kinds of families.

"When you're dealing with a *customer*," I would say, "you've got to be unfailingly polite, unfailingly helpful, and unfailingly patient." It became especially important that no phone call from a student or parent or other family member be mishandled. Though no one quite realized it at the time, academic life had begun to make its transition from the world of "pure print" to the "electronic mode." A parent whose call wasn't sensitively handled could prove to be instrumental in the transfer of an undergraduate to some other institution. And even *that* didn't take account of bad "word of mouth," in which a single mis-handled telephone call could affect the decisions of three or four or five potential students.

—Remarks to the Whitney Center, Hamden, Conn., March 11, 1996

∿

THE ROLE OF FACULTY MEMBERS

One of the most important roles a teacher can play is that of a role model. He or she, regardless of the precise subject matter being taught, needs to serve as an example of a concise and effective communicator—a role that the student, in turn, will have to play many times in his or her own career. The teacher must also serve as a role model when it comes to research.

Those who achieve remunerative and satisfying employment in this society are able to sit down, analyze a problem, do whatever home-work is needed in order to make that analysis as foolproof as possible, and then communicate their conclusions to their superiors. They are, in effect, highly motivated researchers in quest of effective, economic, and elegant solutions. The ability to perform daily research of this kind is obviously a career asset of major dimensions.

—Remarks to the National Center for Academic Achievement
and Transfer Panel, Philadelphia, Pa., October 19, 1992

Those who are most inclined to choose an academic career tend to be more verbally inclined than the average American, more given to criticism and the need for *proof*, and far less likely to accept a pleasing appearance as a substitute for documentable reality. In other words, professors bear some distinct resemblances to lawyers. But whereas lawyers know that all these inclinations must be harnessed to the need to win cases, which in turn means that they win more clients, which in turn means that they have more income, professors arguably are yoked to an ideal of absolute truth, regardless of truth's practical consequences.

The culture that faculty members generate when they gather in an academic setting is unique. While they transact certain obvious administrative necessities during their professional lives—everything implied by departments, by votes, by chairpersons, by deans, and by vice presidents—many don't see those parts of their lives as central to their *real identities*. In between their first inclinations toward higher education and their first full-time jobs, future professors are shaped by their graduate training. And within that training, they are typically subjected to processes of challenge—summed up by the dissertation defense—that can be isolating.

This is followed by a reinforcing process that begins once they are on the full-time payroll of a college or university. They *know* that nothing will advance their careers more quickly and effectively than a nationwide reputation in their individual disciplines. Indeed, the metaphors that dominate their thinking about themselves, once they have become fully committed to an academic career, are *independent* rather than *organizational*, and *heroic* rather than *cooperative*.

To an extent that senior administrators sometimes fail to appreciate, faculty members *do* set the tone and *do* powerfully contribute to the culture of a college or university. The institution of tenure, by its guarantee of longevity, makes them all the more influential in that respect. And right now, the future of total quality management in the higher education sector hinges on whether they can be drawn into its presuppositions and procedures. What seems most unlikely is that a successful "quality-improvement culture" can be developed within an institution of higher learning whose full-time faculty members remain permanently separate from it.

—Remarks at the Mid-Atlantic Convention, Society for College and University Planning, Baltimore, April 15, 1993

REASSESSING TENURE

W here the institution of tenure is concerned, even moderate critics of higher education question whether academic freedom has gone far too far, and is now the cloak regularly donned by those with tenure. Meanwhile, even tenure's most enthusiastic advocates no longer deny that the issue is now centered on *job security*.

—Remarks at the Mitre Corporation's "Distinguished Lecture Series," Bedford, Mass., February 25, 1992

T here was a time when tenure seemed unassailable. Its role in the defense of academic freedom was commonly acknowledged. Even state legislators paid tribute to the fact that today's controversial idea could become tomorrow's staid axiom, and that academicians needed protection from those individuals—including university presidents and ambitious politicians—who for some reason felt hostile toward professors and their thinking.

That "golden age" has now departed, and we are unlikely to see its return. In a nation actively rededicating itself to the principle of universal competition, job security—especially when it is conferred on a "lifetime" basis—sticks in the craw of Americans who are often worrying about their employment.

The American way of life today is built around an entirely new axiom: that the Eighth Deadly Sin, far worse than the other seven, is the sin of feeling (and looking) comfortable. The related forces of insecurity, competitiveness, and accountability are being imposed on every profession and every way of earning a living. State legislators who "talk tough" toward anyone who can be designated as a "freeloader" are themselves being hit with term-limit proposals. The race into new information technologies threatens any business or businessperson who falls even a year behind. Even Social Security and Medicare get bracketed with other questionable "entitlements."

Is it any wonder, therefore, that the traditional pillars of the academy—and tenure most of all—are in the process of wobbling like the Philistine temple at the hands of Samson? Americans have learned to resent those who are comfortable if this comfort is purchased by anything other than inherited wealth, obtained from private sources. Can we feel astonished, therefore, when they and their political representatives scapegoat the allegedly comfortable inhabitants of the academic world, who can ensure their incomes past the age of 70?

To alter this perception would require a remarkable act on the part of American academicians: They would have to forestall "outside forces" by making themselves less professionally comfortable. They would have to impose, on themselves, disciplinary procedures with teeth. The actual number of professors deprived of tenure each year, now a laughable fraction of all those employed in higher education, would rise steadily.

Is self-discipline of this kind even remotely conceivable? Since those who make decisions with regard to tenure are those who already have it, and who therefore share this sense of entitlement, the prospects for "inside" rather than "outside" reform—in higher education as in medicine, banking, and law—would seem to be rather dim. It is urgent that those employed in higher education adopt a tone and perspective that is sensitive to the profound economic insecurity affecting their fellow Americans.

—Excerpted from "What Strategy Should We Now Adopt to Protect Academic Freedom?" in *Academe,* American Association of University Professors, January-February 1996

1 9 9 5

THE "OUTSIDER INSIDER"
EXPERIENCE

REMARKS TO THE HIGH SCHOOL STUDENT CLASS
OF OPERATION UNDERSTANDING, WASHINGTON, D.C., MAY 30, 1995

When university presidents talk to groups of young people like you, they are expected to do two things simultaneously. They're expected to be *inspiring*, to help you feel that you can move forward in life with confidence, energy, and commitment. They're also expected to be *wise* and *informative*, with lots of insights into human history and culture—the kinds of intellectual insights that are worthy of American higher education.

Well, I confess it to you: Being inspiring and intellectual at the same time is no easy task! Most people, when they hear you being analytical and smart, also conclude that you're being *competitive* . . . that you might even be showing off a little . . . and that if they're not at least as smart as you are, then life might turn out to offer them some problems. Meanwhile, those who try to be inspiring had better see to it that the people they're talking to aren't the ones they're competing with. If you're a basketball coach, for example, you want your team competing only with the other team, not with *you*!

So I've done some hard thinking about what I would say to you today, and how I could somehow be inspiring and analytical at the same time. What was there in the history of both blacks and Jews, I asked myself, that could be called both very informative *and* very inspiring? Is there some way in which both groups have had an experience, in their separate histories, that tells us a lot about the human species as it has lived on this planet for several million years, while also encouraging us to feel good and optimistic and determined in our own individual lives?

This is what I've come up with: What blacks and Jews share most of all is the experience of the "Outsider Insider." All human beings, as we know, tend to think of themselves as belonging to certain kinds of *groups*. A single person might feel that he or she belongs to the white group, the American group, the Baptist group, the group known as the wealthy, the group known as midwesterners, the group known as stockbrokers, and the group known as homeowners . . . as well as the groups known as parents, television watchers, *Time* magazine readers, and scrambled-egg lovers!

There's one person who's convinced that he or she belongs to *11* different groups—and even those 11 categories are just for starters. Because after all, you also belong to the group that shops at your particular supermarket, worships at your particular church, and prefers your particular brand of toothpaste.

Of course, belonging to any group means that while you're *inside* it, you're also *outside* all the groups it doesn't represent. The fact that you belong to the Heineken drinkers means you probably don't belong to the Budweiser drinkers. The fact that you belong to those who head for the salad bar probably means that you'd hesitate to join those who like nothing better than a good steak, a baked potato with lots of sour cream, thick crusty bread absolutely dripping with butter, and a nice thick cigar.

You're inside some groups; you're outside other groups. But what do you do if the group that you're inside of is also a group that's been made to feel, over and over again in its history, that its whole mission in life is to be *outside*—that in some curious way it embodies the very principle of alienation, and that those who belong to it mainly share the fact that they are *outsiders*?

Years ago, a very smart man wrote a book called *White Over Black*. The book traced, from about 500 years ago, the idea that whites—always, everywhere, and under all conceivable circumstances—are superior to blacks. That's a belief that's been widely, though not universally, shared by an awful lot of whites living in an awful lot of places, and by a few self-hating blacks as well. It's what you might call a *negative identity*, and what it adds up to is that each time a black person looks in the mirror, he or she is supposed to see someone who by definition is undesirable.

A negative identity of a very similar kind historically has been handed out to Jews. The role assigned to European Jews hundreds of years ago was to testify—by their poverty and their misery and their likelihood of being persecuted and/or killed—to the superiority of the Christian religion and the error they made when they failed to adopt it. A Jew, Europe declared, was nothing less than a walking, talking *mistake*. His or her role in life was to help even the poorest and most miserable Christian feel good by comparison!

Now, considering the negative identities once assigned to blacks and Jews, most folks would say that it's hard to conceive of anything worse. Imagine going through life as someone whose only *inside* is to be *outside*—to be someone who, by definition, can never get beyond being what other people don't want to be! Isn't that the single worst thing that could ever happen to a human being?

Well, yes and no. On one hand, it's certainly an experience you'd want to escape. European Jews like my parents escaped from it, or from the worst parts of it, by coming to the United States. This, they discovered, was actually a country where they had some *rights* guaranteed by the law of the land and enforced by its judicial system. Meanwhile, American blacks, most of whom stayed in the country where they were born, carried out a movement of a different kind. They themselves didn't move, but they moved the *country*! They changed it into being just a little more fair and decent toward those who were, after all, its black *citizens*.

Still, neither blacks nor Jews can completely get past the histories that shaped them. They cannot escape their memories. They know in their bones what it's like to be an *outsider insider*—someone whose role in life is to be *rejected*. And by knowing *that*, they've also learned a very precious truth that, you might say, echoes through the human centuries and the universal human experience.

It's amazing, when you look closely at human history, how people have always insisted on creating heroes and heroines who stand *outside* of their societies. The ancient Greeks, for example, invented a literary form called "Tragedy" whose whole point was that by falling as low as you can fall, you also undergo a certain spiritual *rise*. You step beyond the limits that keep most of your fellow human beings limited and locked in.

In much the same way, the Hebrew prophets declared that the worst moments in the history of the Israelites or Jews, such as when they were exiled from their own land to the distant city of Babylon, were just a prelude to a much better time, when Israelites or Jews would come to have great value for their fellow human beings and would, in fact, become global leaders—and when their religious scriptures would come to have meaning for those living in distant lands.

And surely there's a related phenomenon in the extent to which human beings who aren't black have nevertheless powerfully identified themselves with the black experience. The black experience, it turns out, has its *universal* as well as its *particular* aspect. To watch a single black person coping with, and hopefully overcoming, the negative identity so unfairly *dumped* on him or her . . . to watch a single fellow human being fighting against human injustice . . . is to feel inspired about your *own* life, even if you happen not to be black.

Because it's a fact that for the vast majority of all the human beings who have ever lived, injustice has been a very hard thing to deal with. Most children reach a certain moment in their lives when—suddenly, sharply, and very painfully—they're forced to recognize that injustice is possible, that they can be treated unfairly as well as fairly, and that other human beings are capable of ignoring their pain. That's what it's like to be an outsider insider. As you struggle with your negative identity, you become a positive inspiration.

It's not a great life position to be in. Nobody, if offered a choice, would necessarily jump into it. But once you've found yourself inside it, once you've had to wrestle with its minuses, including its very painful memories extending back hundreds and even thousands of years, you discover its pluses as well. What *you* know is what your fellow human beings so often *yearn* to know. You've had the chance to look at the life all around you from a perspective that isn't limited to just one tiny set of truths or one narrow identity.

I would even draw a parallel between being black or Jewish and getting a college education. One of the hardest tasks college teachers have always faced is how to take a young person from a limited background and get him or her to see life from some altogether different points of view. A young man from suburban Philadelphia has to develop an understanding of life in 19th-century India or 20th-century Japan. A young woman from center-city Chicago has to look through the eyes of an artist who painted a mural in ancient Egypt. A student from abroad—from, say, Singapore or Taiwan—has to learn about the pressures and tensions that an American black takes for granted.

Colleges, in other words, take for granted the role that requires them to get insiders outside. Those who previously took one very limited and defined reality for granted must now climb out of themselves and learn to see themselves from the *outside* as represented by *other* human experiences.

The great advantage of being a black or a Jew is that this maneuver, which many students find so challenging, has something rather natural about it. There's nothing like a period of exile from the human realities all around you to help you understand that those realities are in fact arrangements that can be changed once people decide to change them. And that's a kind of wisdom that can never be taken away from you.

GW AT 175: THE PROGRESS
OF AN ADAPTIVE UNIVERSITY

REMARKS TO THE NEWCOMEN SOCIETY OF THE UNITED STATES,
WASHINGTON, D.C., NOVEMBER 30, 1995

W hat can you say about a university on its 175th anniversary?
In the case of The George Washington University, perhaps it
is that, in at least one critical respect, it remains what it was
in its formative years: a highly *adaptive* institution. And that is fortunate,
indeed, because the University's need to adapt—its ability to change as
circumstances change—is vital to its success, now and in the future.

Founded in 1821, GW was faced early on with the challenges of a
capital city that, like the nation whose federal center it housed, was still
in the process of taking shape. And as the young nation sought to
establish its footing in a new international "marketplace," the
University sought to define its role as America's first truly urban university (and as one whose student population often was mostly part
time and often consisted largely of federal employees). As time went
on, the Civil War and other national developments imposed themselves
dramatically on the University's operations. Financial problems often
threatened to close the place down. In such an environment, a mood of
alert adaptiveness came to be taken for granted by GW's teachers and
administrators. Today that quality is one of our greatest strengths.

As the University continues its quest for national and international
standing, it must acknowledge that the national "higher education scene"
of the 1990s demands much greater attention to marketing and maintenance. Academic standards must be kept rigorous, though not rigid, and
the University must report convincingly about that issue to students and
families, who are becoming increasingly concerned about tuition and fees.
In this connection, information technology, which is essential to campus
efficiency, has become vital to GW's "outreach" programs—including its
efforts to make the public aware of its strengths and accomplishments. As

"customer awareness" increases in higher education, the relationship between pedagogy and economics becomes critical.

One reason students are drawn to GW, regardless of their intended careers, is that the Washington setting is synonymous with "being at the center"—a place where policy-related matters are defined and determined, and where both good and bad news about the national economy tends to arrive and be discussed as early as possible. With Washington as its home town, GW has little choice but to be at least as effective, in terms of its own decisions, as the United States Navy and the World Bank.

Among other things, that means keeping the University in the black while still carefully controlling its tuition, fees, and other charges. Thirty or 40 years ago, when infusions of cash from our federal and state governments were creating the world's first mass higher education system, money was seldom referred to in campus discussions. Dramatic annual increases in revenue were simply taken for granted. Today, on the other hand, as cutbacks in financial support for higher education are routinely debated on Capitol Hill, and as even the most benevolent contributors to GW programs must confront other demands on their generosity, the need to maintain a balanced budget has become imperative.

Also imperative is the need for the University to tell its story to the world, but without engaging in "hype." What GW has done in recent years, therefore, has been to publicize the substance of what it offers and then to let people draw their own conclusions. When international political leaders and creative thinkers become members of our faculty, for example, we have a public relations resource that we scarcely need to inflate. Similarly, the fact that GW has become a major site for deliberations sponsored by the executive and legislative branches of the federal government needs no "pushing." Our university's growing role in American political life is directly connected to the intellectual grassroots in its academic departments, where broad ambitions are translated into specific projects and programs.

At the same time, GW has become highly sensitive to the importance that students attach to their own professional and job-related goals. In a fast-moving international economy like the one that now dominates so many aspects of our lives, few academic decisions are free of "career significance." So while many forces in academic life encourage faculty members to concentrate more on their research than on their students, GW strives, through its Career Center and related efforts, to correct this imbalance. All entrances to the campus could well be engraved with "They're going to have to earn a living."

But no matter how well GW may position itself academically and economically, there are limits to what it can do to influence national sentiment about higher education in general. Clearly the academic world has been in a highly critical and volatile state for well over a decade. As tuitions have continued to rise at colleges and universities across the country, the public has become less and less shy about criticizing the institutions' perceived shortcomings. And this has been accompanied by a desire, more often expressed implicitly than explicitly, to see higher education take on a number of augmented or unprecedented roles.

One growing expectation is that, as universities continue their research agendas, they will also find ways to compensate for the shortcomings of the nation's public high schools. We often hear that high school students in other industrialized countries work more days per year and longer hours each day than their American counterparts, that they do better on tests, and that their teachers hold them to higher standards. But while Americans recognize the need to improve their public schools, our nation has yet to address in any formal way how colleges and universities should go about helping the graduates of those schools compensate for their educational deficiencies.

In effect, it has been left to each institution of higher education, working under the banner of "free enterprise," to increase the number of high school seniors who apply for admission and thus to raise standards by being able to select a smaller (and therefore more worthy) proportion of them. GW has pursued such a strategy with great success. But this very success can also be part of a national failure if higher education collectively determines that it has no place for a growing number of high school graduates in need of remediation.

This is a problem our nation must address, although doing so may prove difficult at a time when there is so much rising sentiment against "interference from Washington." Whatever the virtues of "states' rights," the doctrine does not seem to favor rising graduation standards for secondary schools in all 50 states.

Our colleges and universities also are being urged, meanwhile, to imbue their students with civic and moral values, and to counter the fear that we have become a decadent and immoral society. In a broad sense, to be sure, universities are dedicated to serving the human spirit. They are dedicated to training human intellect, and to strengthening human understanding. But the current mood in our country often goes far beyond a concern about intellect. Perceiving the nation to be in the throes of a moral crisis, the public frequently hungers for ways to strengthen spiritual, rather than intellectual, values.

This mood poses special challenges for higher education. It is already true that our universities, without quite acknowledging that they were doing so, have often provided opportunities for contemplation and for what could easily be described as "spiritual" values. When a class is discussing a novel or a poem or the sermon delivered by a Colonial American clergyman, for example, feelings must often be taken into account if the discussion is to have any meaning. And to take feelings into account, of course, you have to *feel* them!

But as religious and moral and transcendental values have begun to play an increasingly important role in contemporary political and social dialogue, universities are sometimes finding themselves pushed to take a further step. They are being asked to give the proponents of a religiously based morality the same support and recognition extended to advocates of various positions in secular scholarship and natural science. If our society is in a deep moral crisis, the reasoning seems to be, then our universities should "pitch in" to resolve the crisis, especially since they enroll young people preparing to enter the society's work force and to contribute substantially to its daily life.

That, I suggest, is a troubling proposition. Our universities are grounded in a temporal outlook that argues for the *study* of religion and morality, and asks us to act as their host in a generic way. But except in the case of a Catholic university or a Yeshiva university, our academic institutions should not be advancing the tenets of a specific faith. We need to be a home to the non-believer, as well as to the devout. Students who wish to organize spiritual or religious activities on a secular campus should not be prohibited from doing so.

Quite the contrary: In a private institution, every accommodation should be provided to people of all persuasions, including the skeptic. Those with strong beliefs of various kinds should be free to raise, in their classes, the possibility that a lack of strong beliefs is causing our society great or even irremediable harm. Treading the somewhat blurry line between hospitality and advocacy in a secular environment is just one of the difficult challenges higher education must face in our very complicated age!

Then, too, our universities are often being asked to serve the cause of "pan-cultural justice." At a time when affirmative action programs are under attack by leading intellectuals, some of whom have pulled back from earlier commitments to liberalism, universities find themselves in a singularly difficult position. Mainly by default, they still constitute one of the forces in American life most capable of promoting justice—and of seeing to it that the doors of opportunity remain open to men and women of every ethnic group, linguistic group, sexual preference, and race. And this is not an agenda from which they may retreat.

Here again, The George Washington University benefits from its location. Being in Washington, we find ourselves right where the action is in the debate over affirmative action. In this respect, too, GW will continue to adapt its policies and programs to serve the national interest. And as has always been the case since our founding 175 years ago, both equity and fairness will remain at the heart of what we do.

1996

A VISION FOR THE REFORM
OF HIGHER EDUCATION

REMARKS AT THE ANNUAL MEETING OF THE FUND
FOR THE IMPROVEMENT OF POSTSECONDARY EDUCATION,
WASHINGTON, D.C., OCTOBER 26, 1996

At a time in American life when disagreement is all around us, and columnists regularly lament our inability to see things in a common way, there is (unfortunately) *one* subject on which most of us can agree: The nation's colleges and universities are in a crisis. Indeed, whether we look at them from the perspective of a faculty member, administrator, parent, or trustee, our academic institutions often seem to be trapped in a web of interlocking *crises*.

That many institutions are in a *fiscal* crisis goes without saying. While they struggle to hold their annual increases in tuition and fees to a minimum, they continue to be confronted by higher education's labor-intensive budgets, not to mention the oft-deferred and increasingly urgent costs of campus maintenance.

Meanwhile, our colleges often experience crises of morale and Doubt (with a capital "D"), which means that they must deal with questions like these:

❧ Now that the "required courses" of half a century ago are seldom required, what do undergraduates truly and definitely need to learn?
Answer: *The matter is in doubt.*

❧ How do we draw the line between the curriculum as a quest for knowledge and the curriculum as a basis for employment?
Answer: *The matter is in doubt.*

❧ How do we make sure that university graduates with Ph.D.'s don't become candidates for unemployment, underemployment, and malnutrition?
Answer: *The matter is in doubt.*

～ And how, in the relationship between higher education and society, do we rebuild some of the trust and cooperation that were almost taken for granted in the years just after World War II? Answer: *The matter is in doubt.*

Given all this uncertainty, let's return to basics and ask the single most embarrassing question we can: What, in the America of the 1990s, is higher education actually *for*? In other words, how does the academic enterprise respond to the question that the public is throwing at practitioners in virtually every profession these days: "What are we actually *paying* you for—and what can you actually *do* for us?"

I would begin with something of a truism: Americans continue to send their children to postsecondary institutions, and to make financial sacrifices for that purpose, because they want the institutions to *do something* for their kids. That boils down to making their children competitive in the quest for a better life, which is most often defined as a better *economic* life than they could otherwise hope to achieve. Americans expect higher education to produce nothing less than a class transformation—or, if the family is already in the upper-middle-class range, at least a class stabilization.

This sort of transformation doesn't necessarily mandate the death of the liberal arts or the triumph of crude utilitarianism. There will always be a certain number of students whose primary reason for attending college is a desire for knowledge. And besides, people understand the connection between acquiring cultural sophistication and improving one's social status. If you're looking for people to help you with your advancement, you're probably better off conversing with your fellow attendees at the theater than with the person selling you subway tokens.

Yes, Americans know that we live in a college-educated world. Between the American high school graduate and the American college graduate, a much broader gap exists than between our college graduate and his or her counterpart in Stockholm, Milan, or Vladivostok—and this is true even when we allow for the traditional weaknesses of American secondary schools. High levels of literacy, combined with the ability to reason quickly and accurately, are now the basis for admission to a truly internationalized bourgeoisie, which uses brain power with unprecedented speed and, which, to say the least, doesn't suffer fools gladly. Middle-class life has been intellectualized. As institutions that proselytize on behalf of the intellectual functions, colleges and universities have therefore retained or regained their relevance to our society.

So let us consider: If we want to stay relevant, and if we want the public to support us, what kind of higher education system must we develop? To begin to respond to that challenge, we need to be somewhat critical of the mixed messages that we're getting from the public. Higher education's great postwar expansion was often fueled by the nation's defense needs in an increasingly technological world. Higher education thus became identified in American minds as an intellectual *engine* of sorts, spouting the kinds of new discoveries that would (a) keep the Soviet Union at bay while (b) proving that life in our capitalist system was far better, far more satisfying, and much longer lasting than life over there.

By the 1960s, American postsecondary education had moved toward the center of the American economy. Our colleges and universities became true "gatekeepers" for the jobs and careers that kept the economy functional. But while Americans supported the broadest and deepest expansion of postsecondary education the world had ever seen, they proved reluctant to sponsor the related changes we needed in our elementary and secondary schools.

Soon, however, came a major new cliché: The average American high school graduate was arriving at the postsecondary gates as an intellectual invalid in need of emergency treatment before he or she could benefit from a college education. Set an American high school graduate next to his or her European or East Asian equivalent, and the American was a comparative dwarf who lacked fluency in *any* foreign language and seemed shaky even in the use of English.

Soon we witnessed the division of American faculty members into two distinct classes. Working deep in the boiler room, where the equivalent of shoveling coal was the teaching of basic skills, were the academic proletarians whom no one envied. Far above that level lived the full-time, tenured faculty members whose tasks included a sheer minimum in the way of teaching and a well-rewarded maximum in the way of research. And a natural, if mostly unintended, consequence of this value system was to confirm what had begun in the early 20th century—the rise of research over teaching to a dominant position in our academic institutions.

No one ever consciously put teaching *down*. But in a reward system focused on the frontiers of knowledge—one that saw technological triumph as foreign-policy triumph and regarded undergraduates as victims of their previous schooling, teaching slowly but surely lost its original luster, even in the arts and the humanities. Institutions once proud that even their senior professors taught freshman English or freshman humanities courses began switching to harried and underpaid graduate students.

By now this system has given birth to a humorous genre of its own. Families bankrupt themselves to send a son or daughter to Harvard. After all, isn't Harvard the home of many eminent authorities with global reputations? Ask your son or daughter three years later whether he or she ever *saw* one of those eminences, and the answer is likely to be "No." The figure in front of the classroom is usually closer to 26 than 66 years old. The prevailing policies of major universities often turn out, in this research-oriented system, to bear little relationship to the ideals they articulate in their public pronouncements.

In the necessary reform of higher education, therefore, I think the first step should be to explain to the public what we are actually doing to justify the money we charge. We must not only restore teaching to its former status as the very core of higher education. We must also see to it that teaching is developed into a more advanced art than ever before. And what this translates into, in effect, is the kind of teaching that flows *naturally* into research while carrying students along with it to the latest, most exciting aspects of the field in question. Unfortunately, not all faculty members are capable of doing that sort of thing in an engrossing manner.

So we need to succeed in elevating postsecondary teaching to the level of a highly competitive art—one that attracts tangible rewards and that college teachers aspire to master with the energy they now devote to publishing their dissertations. An ethic of teaching as a form of national service must accompany our present emphasis on scholarly publication. And institutions of higher education must learn how to boast about their pedagogical accomplishments, especially as demonstrated by the lives and careers of their graduates—the way they now boast, appropriately, about a Nobel Prize-winning faculty member or the fact that Professor X has written the definitive study of Sumerian verb forms.

Teaching as an intellectual activity, as a form of art, even as a form of magic—*that*, we must somehow convince the American public, is what we do to earn our living. Since we hope that our students will be as bright and as motivated as this kind of teaching can make them, we can expect that sometimes they will press us *hard*. So in order to deal with their restless and inquiring minds, we will have to stay on top of our subjects—always keeping up with the most recent developments and always reaching as far as we can.

As all of this suggests, I see a rededication to teaching as the basis, also, for restoring academic morale. It's not uncommon these days to hear reports of widespread malaise among the practitioners of higher education. This hurts us deeply, because college teachers who feel perpetually "on the ropes" aren't likely to do very well in responding, for example, to the assaults of fundamentalists and creationists, or in convincing students that stretching their minds can be as valuable as stretching their limbs.

But how do we manage to reform higher education in the absence of a truly provocative national emergency? Though we're fortunate not to be faced right now with a Cold War or a world war, surely we recognize how such developments have served in the past to generate regular transfusions of taxpayer money into our colleges and universities. It was enough to give academic employees a sense that the nation really loved them. But what do we do now? How do we make people see that the production of college graduates who cannot compete economically is as serious a threat to the United States as the one posed by nuclear weapons?

That sort of question acquires a special pungency if we acknowledge that the internal politics of higher education often favors an ethic of individual, rather than collaborative or mutual, accomplishment. For faculty members today, what often really matters is their standing within a discipline rather than any sentiments of loyalty toward their own institutions. The one who succeeds at a particular university—who gains tenure, promotion, and an attractive salary—is often the one most ready to leave for another institution. In this highly self-centered system, so many decades in the making, how can we make good teaching one of the most important values?

Such a transformation is possible, it seems to me, only if those who work in postsecondary education develop some of the reflexes that are now taken for granted in the business world. You don't have to read many issues of *The Wall Street Journal* to discover how nervous companies have become in our competitive age, and how much planning they do to prepare for the worst, including the efforts of other companies to steal their customers. The "horror stories" in today's business world affect entire professions, like medicine and law, where a sense of immunity and privilege has given way to a perpetual fear of "what's next?"

Perhaps the best place to begin a reform effort is the point at which our schools and colleges intersect. Recently, in an article on "Those Educated Asians," *The Economist* observed:

"One of the most striking characteristics of countries like Taiwan, Singapore, and South Korea has been their emphasis on raising the educational standards of the whole population rather than the elite. Moreover, those developing countries that invested heavily in primary education have done much better economically than those that concentrated more on university education. In 1960, Pakistanis and South Koreans were about as rich as each other. But whereas just 30 percent of Pakistani children were enrolled in primary schools, 94 percent of South Koreans were. In the mid-1980s, South Korea's GDP per person was three times Pakistan's. Hard as it is to prove a direct connection, the figures are certainly suggestive."

Given the nature of work in a modern society, the importance of education—from kindergarten through graduate school—as a "national cause" is obvious. Surely American success in education can be no less urgent a cause than was the defeat of Hitler or containment of the Soviet Union. Our colleges and universities need to put themselves in the forefront of this new American struggle. They must be willing to help promote a kind of economic nationalism, and to reject claims that such a role is somehow "beneath" them. Only then can we begin to escape all the reports of academic crisis and answer the tough questions about higher education's content, purpose, and place in American society.

SHORT TAKES IV

INTERNATIONAL PERSPECTIVES

What's *right* about our schools of higher education can best be seen from a global perspective. American faculty members and administrators never cease to marvel at the sheer attractiveness of their institutions to students from abroad—young men and women who come here from Asia, from Europe, from Latin America, and from every other continent in order to obtain the skills and training they need for their careers. What we in this country take for granted when we think of a "college" or a "university" strikes the rest of the world as close to miraculous. What's lacking in the other countries' colleges and universities, above all, is an attitude that our institutions promote and encourage: That their purpose is to *serve* their students, to *help* them with their lives and careers, and therefore to *support* the health and competitiveness of the national economy.

—Remarks at the D.C. Jewish Community Center's John R. Risher
Public Affairs Forum, Washington, D.C., May 6, 1993

The teaching of foreign languages to American school children is a major American industry. Starting in high school and continuing into college, every American student is required to spend *years* studying at least one foreign language—most often Spanish or French, occasionally German, and sometimes even Chinese or Japanese. And yet, remarkably few of these young people achieve what, by international standards, would be regarded as fluency in a language other than English. Meanwhile, many of our students regard language classes as a "hassle," a "bore," or a "waste of time."

Why? What's missing in the teaching and learning of foreign languages in this country? And what must educators do to restore this missing element? My view is that American language study lacks a sense of *urgency*. Consider, by way of contrast, the *urgency* with which an American teenager, when applying for his or her first driver's license, *studies* the state-published booklets of laws and regulations that a person must master in order to receive the license.

—Remarks at the X Triennial Conference, International Association of University Presidents, Kobe, Japan, July 1993

Most of our universities count students from abroad among the most important assets supporting their overall budgets. Foreign students usually pay the full cost of their tuition, room, and board. They are usually entranced by the high level of attention that American universities pay to their students' well-being and convenience. And when the foreign students return to their homelands, they often become enthusiastic proponents of American higher education.

—Address to the Secretary's Open Forum, U.S. Department of State, Washington, D.C., November 2, 1997

W(H)ITHER THE HUMANITIES?

Are the humanities too vocational? I'd say that what's wrong with the history of ideas is usually what was right only a short time before. And that seems to me to be as true about the humanities as about any other subject.

It's become a cliché of sorts to distinguish between humanistic subjects, pursued out of a sheer "love of learning," and those likely to help you find a job. Once, the humanities or liberal arts were *exactly* the subjects that helped you find a job and put money in your pocket. But today that previously close connection is bedeviling the humanities. Having previously served as the doorway to power, they are now languishing in a kind of exaggerated backwater, while the mainstream has seemingly been taken over by computer science, information technology, and similar subjects.

Not only do the humanities now seem to have precious little to do with putting money in one's pocket, but in some places a casual allusion to, say, the Norman Conquest of Britain might look like a vocational *handicap*. These days, if you're trying to score a verbal point, you might be better advised to cite Norman Mailer or a recent Hollywood movie. The humanities, in short, having served for centuries as a doorway to power, are now being seen as the sure road to powerlessness.

Talk humanities, and no one understands a word you're saying.

Can we reverse this situation? To do so, we need to build some curricular *bridges*. We need to create linkages between the humanistic fields and those more obviously concerned with actual human behavior—English or comparative literature on one hand, and economics or political science on the other.

For example, perhaps we should discuss the major Greek and Elizabethan tragedies as *political* documents. Might our attempts to teach Plato to undergraduates be placed under a curricular label like "The Problem of Democracy"? There is something about the reverence surrounding humanistic texts that keeps a good many undergraduates from realizing that Plato is even rougher on democratic politicians than the editorials in yesterday's *New York Times*!

—Remarks at the First Annual Mark H. Curtis Memorial Lecture,
Montgomery County (Maryland) Commission on the Humanities, June 12, 1995

In my view, the humanities do have a future, but we're unlikely to get there without a lot of discussion. We might look closely, for example, at the connection between money and art. How have different cultures dealt with the fact that books typically require an investment of money in order to be *published*?

In recent years, we've seen a slew of books on Rembrandt and Picasso and other artists as *marketers* of their own work. How much cross-listing has that intellectual trend actually produced where our humanistic departments and our business schools are concerned? Shouldn't we be seeing many more courses like "The Cultural Entrepreneur" or "Investing in Manuscripts for Fun and Profit"? Humanism, after all, has everything to do with human beings, and human beings have everything to do with *everything*.

If the humanities are to have a future as well as a past, then we will have to learn all over again how much they tell us about ourselves as *real*—which means *messy*—people. Consider: It's 1920, and two typically messy people are looking at a Picasso painting. One can see only the unpopularity of such a work *at the time*. The other plunks down some money, walks off with the painting, and incidentally makes the grandchildren rich. Doesn't that example of capitalism at work deserve at least as much attention as the history of the stock market?

—Remarks at the First Annual Mark H. Curtis Memorial Lecture, Montgomery County (Maryland) Commission on the Humanities, June 12, 1995

We have entered a time in which anti-colonialism and anti-imperialism have become major intellectual forces, and college curricula have been heavily politicized. When some of the traditional humanistic texts *do* get taught these days, it's often in courses explicitly devoted to "exposing" their pro-Western and ostensibly elitist bias.

Meanwhile, traditional humanists howl over the extent to which ephemeral or insignificant texts are taught to freshmen and sophomores "just because they're written by women or blacks." Added to this was the arrival, just a decade or so ago, of "post-structuralism" in general and "deconstruction" in particular, which left many teachers and students with the feeling that a text could mean almost anything— but was unlikely to mean what it seemed to in 1920 or 1930 or 1940. In short, I'm afraid, the "humanities scene" has become rather discouraging.

But at the same time, there appears to be a great *hunger* for the humanities. To be sure, as we experience our incredible Age of Doubt, in which truth seems to flicker on and off like a dying light bulb, the only statement many people trust is that trust is impossible. Every day we struggle with what we believe and why we believe it. And yet, we do seem to feel enormous nostalgia for a time, which lasted well into the 20th century, when it was obvious that major texts had shaped our culture and that our culture was obviously Western.

All around us in today's political and social picture, shouting at the top of one's lungs has become the norm, especially when it can help you wind up in the sound bites on TV news shows. In the average debate, calling your opponent a murderous Nazi is just a warm-up. One of the things we may be experiencing, therefore, is a hunger for classical literary texts in which even the grossest and most frightening behaviors alternate with quiet and therefore enormously powerful "effects."

When we open the pages of Dante, Shakespeare, Voltaire, or Tolstoy, the qualities we expect are subtlety, nuance, surprise, insight, and revelation. The fact that people keep returning to those texts suggests how inexhaustible and how unhyperbolic they are.

—Remarks at the Community College Humanities Association's National Conference, Washington, D.C., November 10, 1995

What place should the humanities have in community colleges? After all, the vitality of the American community college and its imitators in other countries is based on service to local, regional, and national economies. It draws students who are specifically interested in acquiring vocational skills that point toward stable careers. And what a community college must achieve in only two years would seem to leave very little space for anything as non-vocational as an effective humanities program.

At many liberal arts colleges, after all, humanities programs have taken as long as two years just to "lay the foundation." But we need to help community college students understand that, once they've entered a viable career path, their efforts to "move up" are likely to put them in competition with the graduates of liberal arts colleges where the humanities are taken for granted—or even with high school and college graduates from other parts of the world, where education standards may have been a lot tougher than those that prevail in the United States.

—Remarks at the Community College Humanities Association's National Conference, Washington, D.C., November 10, 1995

Looking back to John Dewey, we encounter the most embarrassing fact about the "student rebellion" of the 1960s: that for all of its ranting and raving, and for all of its mindless destructiveness, it was in many ways driven by the same deep-seated American values that Dewey himself summarized. When the "student radicals" asked why there weren't more blacks and Hispanics sitting beside them in class . . . when the radicals asked why history was usually taught in terms that ignored the side-effects of Western colonialism . . . when they demanded more "relevance" in the postsecondary curriculum . . . they sounded a lot like John Dewey on some sort of a "drug high."

—Address to the Secretary's Open Forum, U.S. Department
of State, Washington, D.C., November 2, 1997

EDUCATION AND TECHNOLOGY

The University—my university—has no choice: It has to spend millions of dollars to enhance the connectivity of the campus, bring it up to the state of the art, put computers on all faculty members' desks, and train them so they can use computers not only for research but also for teaching. We should do this lest we appear like Luddites—and because it's being done everywhere else.

But that doesn't mean I don't worry that we could let ourselves be overwhelmed by form rather than substance and end up using technology to replace thinking. We should not rely on quick fixes or forget that it takes hard intellectual work to be a student or faculty member.

—Interview at The George Washington University, February 2, 1998

EDUCATION BEFORE COLLEGE

The fact that Americans have started viewing even primary education from a "pre-collegiate perspective" is having more and more of an impact on the rest of the world.

It's an easy impulse to caricature: The upper-middle-class American who is frantic about getting his or her child into the right nursery school—the one that leads to the right elementary and secondary schools, which in turn lead to The George Washington University or, perhaps as a fallback, to Harvard—seems made-to-order for a play by Molière.

But the consciousness of how national educational culture gets shaped—and how it connects with the kinds of economic strength that support individual self-development, which reinforces national economic strength in an international marketplace—is shared by legions of professionals in such areas as public health, women's affairs, and economics. For example, we are now experts at assessing how a community college system must face two ways at the same time. For students bound for employment, it is a "terminal" system with two-year degrees. But for a significant number of other students, it is a transitional phase as they prepare to go on to four-year colleges and perhaps even to graduate school.

—Address to the Secretary's Open Forum, U.S. Department
of State, Washington, D.C., November 2, 1997

It's at least a tenable hypothesis these days that a "college-level awareness" is percolating down into all of our pre-collegiate systems. In part that's a result of computerization—the introduction of the Internet into even the least favored schools in America's inner cities. In part it represents growing parental awareness. And in part it's a result of efforts by colleges and universities themselves to spread the word about higher education and to attract students not only from their own communities and other parts of the United States, but also from other nations.

—Address to the Secretary's Open Forum, U.S. Department
of State, Washington, D.C., November 2, 1997

EDUCATIONAL OPPORTUNITY

It simply won't do to have a society where all the well-paying jobs are held by one cohort, particularly when that group is distinguishable by color and race. That seems to me to be a recipe for revolution. And since I am among the more conservative of men, I think that in order to protect the society that we've crafted, and to let it continue to flourish, we've got to find a way to distribute enough opportunity and wealth across racial and socioeconomic barriers, among others, to make the American dream a continuing possibility.

But if you have, as we do, large numbers of people, especially among African Americans, who think there is no hope for them and or their children, then I think you've got a real social problem. The University needs to use its resources to the extent that it can, without compromising its own programs, to work with elementary and secondary schools—and their teachers—to increase their educational effectiveness. And the University should work to enhance the city in which it is located and whose beneficiary it is in terms of tax exemptions and other benefits.

—Interview at The George Washington University, February 2, 1998

For most of my professional career, the issue of race and reconciliation between the races, and between the African American community and the rest of America, has been part of my agenda. And I'm never sure whether I ought to be cheered by what we have accomplished or depressed by what has not yet been done.

What depresses me now is we seem to be off in a debate about nomenclature. The truth of the matter is, I'm not for or against "affirmative action"—as far as I'm concerned, that's merely a phrase. If "affirmative action" offends, I'm prepared to jettison the phrase. What I do care about is *justice*—and the always daunting problem of distributing limited opportunities and limited goods.

And I don't want my kids going to all-white schools. They don't live in an all-white world—and if they are going to school to learn how to live in this world, their schools need to look something like this world.

At the same time, I don't want to see us abandon empirically driven measures of accomplishment. We need accountability, and we need to reward and celebrate hard work and achievement. If affirmative action means that less capable people get opportunities while more capable people are left sitting on the sidelines, that's a problem. In that sense, nobody wants affirmative action for brain surgeons or airplane pilots. So I come back to my notion that we have to seek justice.

Perhaps we should rename affirmative action since the very words seem to provoke certain people who might otherwise be sympathetic to its goals. I don't think advocates of affirmative action care much what it's called. What they seek is perhaps known by an old-fashioned word—justice. We don't have to talk about less capable people denying opportunities to more capable people. We need to be more imaginative in defining capacity. During the course of my life, I've met very few people who were outstanding at everything. And I've met an even smaller number who weren't quite remarkable in their own ways. Americans have an instinctive capacity for fairness. They know when things aren't equitable, and left to their own devices, they try to put things right. There is an impulse in this country for decency. We need to trust it more often.

—Interview at The George Washington University, February 2, 1998

1 9 9 7

THE CONSEQUENCES
OF "THINKING MARKETABILITY"

REMARKS AT A SEMINAR OF THE INSTITUTE FOR EDUCATIONAL
LEADERSHIP, WASHINGTON, D.C., MARCH 21, 1997

T he first word that popped into my head as I began preparing these remarks was *money*. For most academic institutions, money often appears to be a compulsion. On one hand are the costs of actually *providing* higher education—costs that tend to move relentlessly upward. Faculty and staff members expect regular raises, maintenance costs have a similar tendency to rise, and the folks running the admissions office are the first to howl if the shrubbery isn't kept neat or if broken stretches of sidewalk aren't repaired. The result is a budget that relentlessly traces an always-larger-this-year-than-last-year escalation in the cost of chalk, pencils, computers, telephone calls, toilet paper, elevators, books, videotapes, vacuum cleaners, dishwashers, and—well, you get the idea!

So on one hand, we have all these costs. On the other hand, we have an American public that's often outraged by the size of the check that has to be written before an accepted applicant can become an enrolled student.

A few decades ago, money was seldom a topic of heavy discussion. Our federal and state governments were providing the most enormous financial support system for higher education that any nation had ever enjoyed. This enabled universities, especially those in the public sector, to grow to unprecedented size. It also created a community college network that added a whole new dimension of education. And no longer was college teaching regarded as synonymous with "genteel poverty."

In more recent years, that has all moved into reverse. Government support seems more and more grudging, and academic institutions must raise a steadily growing percentage of the money they spend just to keep things stable. If the food in the residence halls declines even a bit in quality or quantity, if the library's computers spend too much time "out of order," if a single tile happens to fall from a rooftop and shatter where people can see it . . . if any of those things happen, then you can be sure the critics will be in an uproar. There will be angry letters to the university's president and to campus publications. Soon editorials in the community newspaper will lambaste the institution for so obviously failing in its mission.

When a profit-making corporation experiences problems like that, it adopts a very simple strategy: It raises its prices. But that's not an option that colleges and universities can exercise except with great caution. So we are beginning to see these institutions transform themselves into marketing mechanisms. Having spent many years *resisting* popular pressures, they have changed course and have begun trying to give the public what it supposedly *wants* and is *willing to pay for*. The major policy issues facing higher education thus resolve themselves, ultimately, into one big issue: How to sort out the pressures, tensions, paradoxes, obstacles, and occasional opportunities represented by that new species known as "the marketable university."

When universities practice effective marketing, traditions start to fall. Come to think of it, the universities of yesteryear look, in retrospect, like *counter*-marketing arrangements. Consider the old traditions that, until quite recently, they actively sought to play:

Archaic Tradition No. 1: The tradition that knowledge is valuable for its own sake.

It's no mere coincidence that the word "university" bears an obvious kinship to "universal." At some point in the European Renaissance, it became clear that the world of knowledge was so large that it could survive only if all of its parts were transmitted by institutions of some kind. Thus universities became places where one could study French literature *and* Sumerian history *and* Sanskrit *and* Old Norse *and* nuclear physics *and* Pre-Columbian architecture *and* adolescent psychology *and* the development of Armenian nationalism *and* the migration patterns of the Goths *and* the precise way in which Bismarck convinced the Kaiser that it was time to declare Germany an empire.

On rare occasions, someone would have the bad taste to observe that the advanced seminar in Arctic zoology had an average registration of two students, not counting the professor of zoology assigned to teach it. Such appalling concessions to gross materialism were generally ignored. It made perfect sense, back then, that Professor X should be paid close to $100,000 per year in order to instruct a grand total of nine students. Wasn't he also doing some research?

In that naive age, a department no sooner spotted a new subject on the horizon than the request went out in its annual budget proposal—

someone, somehow, had to be hired in order to teach *that* subject. Otherwise, the members of the department, at their discipline's annual convention, would actually have to *blush* and *stammer* when someone asked whom they had hired to teach the brand-new subject that was sweeping all before it from coast to coast. And what was a university president for—indeed, what was the entire board of trustees for—if not to see to it that professors never had to *blush* or *stammer*?

Now turn your gaze to the university of 1997 as it strives to become a marketable organization. It actually makes a habit of asking how much things cost and whether, if the cost is high, they are worth doing. And it inevitably notices that, while there are subjects that students are *dying* to take, there are other courses to which they are mainly or entirely indifferent. So a university of this kind necessarily turns its back on the ancient tradition that it must teach *everything*. And its president may well say to the board of trustees: "To hire a full-time person who will teach Archaic Macedonian epigraphy . . . given the fact that there are only three specialists in the United States with Ph.D.'s in the subject . . . will cost us at least $160,000 in salary plus benefits. Surely it would be a lot more feasible, when a student absolutely *has* to achieve proficiency in this field, to send that student to another institution in this country or in Europe—perhaps even in Macedonia—where it is already being taught. The Macedonian Ambassador's office tells me that six months of study in his country for one student, including room and board, will cost us about $11,000."

So one consequence of developing a marketable university, which can afford to put some real money into selling services that its faculty members can offer, is to say goodbye to the tradition that a *university* should also be a *universality*. It was a grand idea while it lasted. Which brings me to . . .

Archaic Tradition No. 2: The tradition that universities should solve the big American problem that how much money you have often determines what you can buy.

In the balmy years when money was not a problem, our country experienced a whole new current of thought. Had it been expressed in one sentence (which it usually wasn't), it would have read: "No student in the United States should ever be denied higher education because he or she can't afford to pay for it."

The next step should have been obvious. An amendment to the Constitution, after stating this principle, should also have guaranteed that the federal government would pay the tuition and fees for every such student, leaving to the universities themselves the actual task of instruction and the actual granting of a degree. But for some reason, no such amendment was ever drafted or brought to a vote. Instead, universities were quietly redefined as charitable organizations untainted by materialism—organizations not unrelated to CARE and the Red Cross.

And did they ever try to play the role! "Need-blind admissions" became a fetish of sorts: First universities admitted a student; only *then* did they ask whether he or she had any money to contribute. Had the president of Chrysler or General Motors proposed that cars be given away to those who needed them but couldn't afford to pay for them, the executioner would have had to rush in on roller skates. But universities, vaguely regarded as the inheritors of the medieval church and its charitable ideals, came to be seen as places that could always scrape up some additional cash to compensate for the four or five hundred students who had no money of their own.

Saying goodbye to that particular tradition is also, I needn't tell you, traumatic. When I'm told that someone isn't coming, or coming back, to my own institution because he or she *can't afford to*, a spasm of real pain shoots through my heart. And it's only after I've calmed down that I find myself reflecting on just how important my university is to all the people on its payroll, as well as to all the merchants who like to be paid for the goods and services they have provided. Every year we spend millions of dollars to provide scholarships to students from less-than-privileged backgrounds, but we still don't claim to be doing more than is humanly possible. And in that respect, we're typical of most other American universities in this increasingly tough-minded age, in which a *Democratic* President of the United States has been the one to set national limits to welfare.

Archaic Tradition No. 3: The tradition that, in the area of marketing, universities should function like a cross between a four-year-old child and a visitor from a time before the printing press.

Whatever universities were, in this tradition, they were the opposite of—you should only pardon the expression—"Madison Avenue." Out there in the crude commercial world, the lowest kinds of manipulators created documents called *advertisements*, which were gross attempts to convince people to buy your *product*. Universities, fortunately, were exempted from that. People seeking knowledge—people, in other words, who were seeking *higher* rather than *lower* things—would come to the university because that was where knowledge had always been kept safe.

This particular tradition did quite nicely during the years when Uncle Sam seemed to be emptying his pockets for the sake of the academy. But the tradition began to suffer when university presidents found themselves worrying, just like *business people*, about how to meet the payroll or where to find the money to buy the latest technological equipment. And it didn't help when the Baby Boom was followed by the Baby Bust, and there were fewer and fewer high school seniors to go around.

Grudgingly at first, and then at an accelerating pace, colleges and universities began to adapt to the need to actually *market* their services. One institution would hire a design firm that could actually work with more than one color. Another would hire a director of university relations who actually had some skill in developing contacts in the news media. It became acceptable, even fashionable, for academic institutions to admit that they were—please hold your breath—*competing with other institutions for students*. As the history of ideas long ago testified, the fact that something is *obvious* doesn't necessarily mean that a particular cultural subgroup believes it to be true. Universities had long gotten used to behaving as if they represented, like the publishing industry, an "occupation for gentlemen and ladies." Having spiritually risen far above the idea of competition, they could scarcely admit that they were practicing it where potential students were concerned. By now, they know a lot better.

Meanwhile, as they adapt to all the changing mythology, universities also learn to answer this fundamental question: "What must we teach, and what must we do, to prepare our students to earn a good living in the world economy?" The answers are actually part of academic marketability. Our institutions must make basic decisions about such things as revising the curriculum, developing alternatives to faculty tenure, and giving students better career guidance. All those decisions will revolve around the need to create and maintain a marketable university—a university whose costs are under control, whose virtues are well presented to a broad public, whose instructors are dedicated to teaching as well as research, and whose facilities and resources (especially in the technological realm) are well maintained and up to date. Such a university will go out of its way to reward talented faculty members, administrators, and staff members, while making certain that no one is disgracefully underpaid. And it will serve its students as a role model for entrepreneurship—as an institution that doesn't automatically reject an idea just because it has never been tried before.

In this mission, I have no doubt, our colleges and universities will come through with flying colors.

WHAT I LEARNED FROM MY SON WHO JUST GRADUATED FROM COLUMBIA

REMARKS AT THE ANNUAL DINNER MEETING OF THE
COLUMBIA COLLEGE CLUB OF WASHINGTON, D.C., JUNE 10, 1997

A gathering like this always has a strong philosophical appeal. We're drawn together, obviously, by our memories of a specific school. That's the *communal* aspect. But we're also affected by an *individual* consideration, otherwise known as the course of each of our lives. Columbia College is what launched us. And now, as each of us looks back at that launching, we also weigh what we went on to *do* with it—and the roles it has continued to play in our lives and careers.

These thoughts have been especially poignant for me because Adam Trachtenberg, the elder of my two sons, graduated from Columbia this year. Watching his growth and development as a student necessarily has brought my life full circle. As I observed him living through his years as an undergraduate, I was of course reliving my *own* college years . . . and in the process, I was learning a number of unexpected lessons.

Chief among these, I think, was a lesson about the modern cult, which is partly American but also global, of "The Decline and Fall." Long before Edward Gibbon began to write his remarkable history, our species had produced many works suggesting that life used to be better in "the old days," and that all around us we could see how badly the present compared with the past. Back *then*, of course, the world was experiencing an Age of Gold rather than our own Age of Iron or Age of Bronze. Back *then*, the males were more heroic by far, and the women far more beautiful. And back *then*, it goes without saying, people spoke in magnificent poetry, while today they could only stammer in barely articulate prose. So when my son started at Columbia as a freshman, my expectations had a certain pessimistic quality.

After all, during *my* days at Columbia the place was absolutely stuffed with brilliant teachers and scholars. Jim Shenton was regularly wowing the students in Hamilton Hall. They sat transfixed as he summoned up the texture and the personalities of American history. Up on the fourth floor, Andrew Chiappe was weaving his magic around *The Complete Works of William Shakespeare*, in a voice whose blend of America and England seemed to be the voice of Western civilization itself. Lionel Trilling was giving his students advance notice about his next book of highly influential essays. And down on Broadway, at the West End Bar and Grill, all the ideas being developed at the college met all of the ideas under development "downtown"—ideas that tended toward a glorious radicalism, which frightened away mere mortals but set fires of aspiration under those seeking higher levels of revelation.

Imagine my amazement, therefore, when Adam Trachtenberg, my very own son, seemed to be learning very similar lessons from Freshman Humanities and his other introductory courses. Yes, they were still using the Richmond Lattimore translation of the *Iliad*, rather than a more recent one. And I could see why they were doing that. It was because Lattimore, while translating accurately, was never translating expressionistically. Those who absolutely *insisted* on learning Homeric Greek would always find Lattimore ideal as a helpful "crib." And my son's progress through the Western tradition, as was the case back in the 1950s, covered all of the subjects that continue to agitate each day's newspaper and each decade's political disputes.

So one of the most important lessons I learned from my son was that, contrary to what a lot of folks believe these days, the liberal arts are as relevant as ever. Even if today's undergraduates are likely to write their term papers on computers rather than manual typewriters, they are writing about our cultural reflexes even more than our cultural history. When Virgil describes the defeat of Antony and Cleopatra by Augustus, he sounds all the racist notes with which we are still struggling today. On the other hand, when Shakespeare picks up the same theme, he comes close to declaring that "black is beautiful." And we are left to discuss, and perhaps to decide, whether a grim focus on order is worth the surrender of spontaneity—and whether a decade like the 1960s should be read in essentially Shakespearean terms.

I watched my son as he reaped the familiar benefits of a Columbia education. I admired, yet again, the combination of discipline and intellectual seductiveness with which the college does its work. And I found myself running an unexpected risk—the risk of feeling that life on Morningside Heights had been stored away in a kind of freezer, and that nothing had really changed.

And did *that* lead me to an amazing lesson! When it came time for Adam to choose a major, he walked right past the literary and historical emphases that were so typical of the 1950s. He chose not English literature or French poetry or British history, but mathematics. And then he did something even more amazing. Back in the 1950s, when you decided to major in history or political science, you didn't expect that your studies would have *anything* really straightforward to do with finding a job. After you'd finished law school, perhaps, or an Ivy League Ph.D.—*then* the time would hopefully arrive when someone with a salary to pay would look favorably at *you*, a hard-working ex-student in quest of a salary to earn.

But Adam taught me my lesson. Clubbing together with four other computer-type students, he helped start a company that soon attracted the attention of a much larger company. And what the larger company did, in effect, was to subsidize my son's company to an extent that sent my eyebrows zooming up toward the top of my head. This "kid," as I used to call him, is now a vice president pulling in an impressive salary. And I keep looking in the mirror and asking myself how much credit I can legitimately take for aiding the birth and development of this splendid young phenomenon.

So a Columbia-style liberal arts education in the 1990s, for all its continuity with what you and I experienced, is no bar to moving into Information Technology. Indeed, it may actively facilitate that process. So when you and I look back at what Columbia did for us and how we used the college, perhaps we should allow for its non-stop emphasis on *exactly* the subject of information. You said you were "doing a term paper," but typically you began by examining the raw material from which every term paper had to be built—texts, illustrations, or other artifacts that stretched back to the time when Voltaire or Hobbes or Michelangelo or Thucydides were still alive. Where did those artifacts come from? Who had assembled them, and in what form? How did you know you could trust the form in which they had reached both Butler Library and your own hands? And was that true when you used a translation from another language?

And Columbia didn't just teach history; it taught the *history* of history. For those writing a term paper on a subject of the pre-Gutenberg era, Columbia taught all kinds of lessons about why certain texts were copied and recopied while others fell by the wayside, so that we only glimpsed their titles in some other ancient text. For those tracking a Shakespearean text from its origins to the First Folio, it soon opened all the vistas of Elizabethan publication, right down to the literary thieves who surreptitiously took down the text of a play in shorthand and then issued it in a quarto all their own. The modern phenomenon known as the "quick buck" had a precise Elizabethan counterpart: the "quick shilling." And the fact that Shakespeare attracted so many pirates helped confirm his role as the most popular playwright of his time—as well as an author for *all* time.

The process that gave birth to a math or computer science major at Columbia could therefore be seen as a natural outgrowth of the one experienced by those who went there in the 1950s. And the fact that the word *information* was seldom used in those days to describe our studies did not mean we weren't being thoroughly exposed to the *theory* of information. Butler Library, which looked so solid when we first arrived on campus, became a lot less so after we'd spent a couple of years in its vicinity. Gone were the juveniles who had accepted the high school textbook as the final authority on "what you had to know." Now the question was: "What's the latest poop on whether this text is any good?" If we naively cited a dubious edition in support of a scholarly argument, we had only ourselves to blame when the teacher told us so in a marginal annotation.

As you all know, I'm a Columbia College alumnus who is trying very hard to play the role of a university president. I'm necessarily exposed, therefore, to all of the wars being waged on the subject of Western civilization versus the rest of the world's civilizations. And I don't even want to count the number of manifestoes I've read that regard the words "Western civilization" as tantamount to an act of aggression. A focus on "dead white European males," we're told, is just another imperialistic effort to claim our innocent minds. Books written the day before yesterday, by people totally outside the humanities curriculum, are supposed to be more relevant than those produced by a lot of ancient guys in bed sheets.

Well, one thing I've learned from my son is that you've got to start *somewhere*. I suppose there were at least a few people walking around in the Roman Forum who felt sick and tired of being dominated by a bunch of . . . you should only pardon the expression . . . *Greeks*. Had we been there, we might have heard them mumbling: "*More* Achilles, *more* Odysseus. I'm just sick and tired of all that worn-out irrelevance. What's that got to do with running an *empire*?"

I suppose we should be grateful to Virgil for not listening to stuff like that. And then we probably should be grateful to those who run Columbia College for not revising its freshman and sophomore curriculum to feature the literary work of Bill Gates, the movies of Madonna, or the philosophy of Rupert Murdoch.

As my son Adam develops new computer products, he will be better served by his mastery of the amazing sequence connecting Homer and Dante with Shakespeare and Tolstoy. That sequence also lays the intellectual foundation for understanding the development of Buddhist literature and art from its origins on the Indian Subcontinent to China and Japan.

Indeed, one of the enduring facts about our culture is how it continually resurrects its past as it struggles toward its future. Norman Mailer's latest novel is an autobiography of Jesus. A recent bestselling novel entitled *Alias Grace* was based on a murder trial in 19th-century Canada. And each time we open our morning newspaper and read the latest news from the Middle East, it comes surrounded with visible and invisible footnotes. Has an archaeologist discovered, beneath a certain stretch of land, an inscription bearing the name of a king who lived three thousand years ago? Then its authenticity will soon be questioned by those laying claim to the same stretch of territory three thousand years later.

What I learned at Columbia in the 1950s, what my son learned there in the 1990s, and what each of you learned there during your own years as undergraduates is how the past, present, and future are always in a tumult in relation to each other. No sooner have we settled on a version of what's most relevant to our lives than the revisionists go to work.

Thomas Jefferson's works are made available in the Library of America only moments, it seems, before the suggestion is made that we should stop reading him altogether. We're barely done admiring the handsome edition of Joyce's *Ulysses* in our personal library than a computer-based study announces that it's a mess of misprints. And the minister preparing a sermon must get past a committee of Bible scholars who pronounce 80 percent of the words attributed to Jesus to be fabrications composed by editors.

For political purposes, it's always comforting to suggest that Western tradition is a kind of temple, rising stone upon stone into a perpetually blue sky. Which of us wants to confront the notion that Western tradition is more like a mixmaster, eternally plowing under what seemed, only a little while ago, to be immortal and unchallengeable? All of us work so hard just to earn a living. All of us would like a bit of rest. Why can't Western tradition be a comfortable mattress upon which we can simply flop down with a sigh of relief?

But my son has taught me a different lesson. He came through a Columbia College education with all of his future-oriented faculties intact. Somehow his awareness of Greeks and Romans and Elizabethans and Moderns has fed right into his working position on the cutting edge of the computer field. So I myself will try to cut through false modesty, and will interpret my capacity to be a university president in a similar fashion.

The moment will come, I know, when someone will confront me in my Washington office and tell me that my institution owes some group or other a lot of money—and an even larger amount of respect. But I will control my feelings and resist the temptation to get physical. Perhaps I'll reflect on some moment out of Thucydides, or an especially pungent aphorism by Pascal, or something from Ibsen or Strindberg, and it will help me take hold of myself and come up with the calm statement that the situation calls for. And when I tell my wife all about it at the end of the day, it will be in a spirit that says, in effect: "Like our son Adam, I was lucky enough to study some of life's hardest lessons before they started beating me over the head!"

1 9 9 8

THE POWER IN WASHINGTON
COMES FROM
A SURPRISING SOURCE!

KEYNOTE ADDRESS AT THE "PRESIDENTIAL CLASSROOM FOR YOUNG
AMERICANS" SEMINAR, WASHINGTON, D.C., FEBRUARY 1, 1998

In a way, my talk today is about how my talk today came about. I ask your indulgence as I try to convey the essence of this without becoming overly "clever." You see, there I was—talking with myself about *you*.

"I know they're here to see Washington," I said, "but wouldn't it be more accurate to say that Washington is here to see them?"

"That's interesting," I replied. "You're suggesting that the politicians are already paying a lot more attention to these people than they may know."

"Nicely put," I said to myself. "And these young Americans may also need to know that Washington is frequently on the receiving end of parental anxieties across the nation. And when parents face problems involving their children, they often call or write to political leaders."

"Yes, exactly," I responded. "There is what you might call 'the youth element' here in Washington—a hidden sub-stratum that supports a lot of other issues. Suppose, for example, that Congress is considering a bill aimed at getting the pigeons out of our nation's parks. Would the Senate and the House be kind enough, please, to finance a $3 million study on how this goal can be humanely but effectively achieved? Soon Senator X, whose only ecological credentials consist of the fact that his wife belongs to a garden club, is verbally walloping Senator Y for cosponsoring a measure that would probably end up poisoning millions of innocent birds. Senator Y responds with a litany of citations from the medical literature of the entire planet, all to prove beyond a shadow of a doubt that pigeons carry more disease and destruction from place to place than the 10 plagues that God once rained down on Pharaoh's Egypt."

"So the members of the Presidential Classroom," I continued in this conversation with myself, "would be quite right to buttonhole me and say: 'What do pigeons have to do with anyone under the age of 20?' And I'd have to explain that. 'Senator X isn't saying just what he seems to be saying,' I would point out. 'There's an unspoken subtext here, too, that won't appear in the *Congressional Record*. It consists of the eternal American question: 'What will this do to (or for) our children? If we end up murdering millions of pigeons, won't the backers of this bill be held responsible for damaging the moral values of an entire generation of Americans?'

"Meanwhile, you realize, what Senator Y is saying—about all the terrible diseases that pigeons are allegedly capable of transmitting— also is linked to concerns about young people. 'Take a walk with your kid in one of this country's parks,' goes his unspoken thought, 'and don't be surprised if you end up with a son or daughter who is certifiably dead.' "

Let me move on from this recounting of a conversation with myself by underscoring the fact that politicians are ever mindful of the power of young people. When politicians say "Our world is getting worse," what they usually mean is that it is getting worse for our innocent children. Similarly: "Our world is getting better" suggests that our children won't be ashamed of us for having loused things up so badly.

So, we have a situation here in Washington in which power has a perpetually paradoxical aspect. Power in Washington, I'm happy to inform you, is power to do what politicians' constituents really want them to do. Quite often, it means that official-type people do things their constituents don't even *know* they want, but they'd better be right about that. And after the deed is done, if their constituents are happy, then they're considered smart politicians.

Virtually all of official Washington—certainly the legislative and executive branches, and perhaps even part of the judicial branch—is trying to figure out how Americans are thinking right now. And while they come up with all kinds of strange answers to that question, some of them demonstrably wrong, no one ever doubts for a moment that: Children, alias kids, alias "those young people out there," are right in the middle of most Americans' thoughts and feelings. Let me suggest why that is so.

One reason is that our country has always been associated with an image of joyful infancy, childhood, and adolescence. We actually live under a democratic government that probably is the oldest in the world. When it comes to democracy, other countries, which have tried to learn from the American example, are the real youngsters. Some of them can date their current democratic systems to the end of World War II or the end of the Soviet Union. So why do most inhabitants of Planet Earth keep associating the United States of America with this image of a smiling kid in a T-shirt and sneakers? And why do most Americans agree with them?

The answer, I think, has something to do with America's origins. We came along at a point in history when Europeans and Latin Americans were doing the previously unthinkable: They were taking the sovereigns of their own sacred nations and, metaphorically or even literally, chopping their heads off. But all those potential revolutionaries of the 18th and 19th centuries were nervous. They wanted to get rid of a monarchy, but would the replacement be better? Would it work? Perhaps, they feared, they would end up with a tyranny. The United States of America got there just in time to help those folks feel a bit more courageous. And that, in my opinion, helps to explain why Americans are still perceived by much of the world as harbingers of eternal youth. Which, in turn, means that *you* are seen by Washington politicians and your other fellow citizens as *super*-Americans whose opinions are tremendously important.

Another reason is that, when you look inside the average person's head, you're likely to find some version of the eternal struggle known as "youth versus experience." In most people's minds, the urge to be innovative, daring, and perhaps even revolutionary is always wrestling with the desire to be stable, predictable, and comfortably boring. Put 100 unrelated people in a room, let them get a big argument started on almost any subject, and in a few minutes they'll be choosing up sides. One team, inevitably, will represent fresh, courageous ideas that no one has ever taken seriously before, and the other team will represent solid, traditional thinking.

Now it's bad enough to be in a room in which the 50-year-olds are fighting the 60-year-olds in the name of youthful experiment. But when most adults see people who happen to be *your* age, they get *very* nervous. To them, you seem to reflect the forces of innovation *in their own minds*. Yet they also worry about the risk of turning into caricatures of aging rigidity, always ready to squash a new idea. And so you, without ever having asked for it, are suddenly the stars of a Greek drama. The old Titans are attacked, and eventually overcome, by the more refined gods and goddesses. But no sooner do the gods and goddesses take over than they find themselves having to maintain law, order, and civil peace. At which point the forces of innovation and change, which they themselves represented a short time before, are precisely what they must now question. So that is part of why Washington keeps such a close eye on you. You are seen as allegorical figures in an eternal and *internal* human drama.

Most people who get to be presidents, senators, and members of the House of Representatives do so by defeating at the polls those who preceded them in those positions. They played a symbolically youthful role, claiming that if you voted for them all kinds of presumably not-so-good things would change. When they came to power, they found that they liked it. They liked having nice offices, respectful assistants, and reporters who always wanted to know what was on their minds. So now they may well imagine versions of their earlier selves confronting the politicians they have since become.

But the most important reason that power in Washington is so closely related to our attitudes toward children is that Americans take their national government seriously. They have an underlying faith in the governmental process. And they expect the government to be capable of helping with almost any problem—especially if the problem involves the eternal struggle between children and parents, youth and age, innovation and experience.

One of your reasons for being in Washington is to learn how people here actually *work*—what goes on behind all those marble walls. But you, by being here, are working, too. The people who look at *you* while you are watching *them* are looking at power—the enormous power of the future. Given how Washington thinks, power here is the power of the Presidential Classroom, which is studying with an open mind how the folks in this city are earning or failing to earn their salaries.

As a university president, I experience each day, on a personal level, a lot of what I've been saying to you today. When I meet with other administrators, faculty members, and those who maintain our campus, most of our talk is about students—whether we're serving them as well as we can, whether they're likely to be saying good things about us to their parents and friends, and whether our policies are working for the students' benefit. Am I therefore wielding power? Or is power being wielded over *me*? Those who teach political science or government at my university will probably agree with me that the surest sign that you're powerful is that other people pay close attention to you.

You are here as much to be looked at as to look. You are very important to the important people you are being exposed to. And as I cast my eyes upon you, I have to put some limitations on myself and on what I say. How tempted I am to turn this talk into a commercial on behalf of The George Washington University. I'd love to go on and on about what a terrific place it is, and how beautifully located it is, right in the middle of Washington's most powerful institutions. But I won't give in to that temptation because I don't want you to leave here thinking, "Hey! That Trachtenberg guy sounded desperate! His university must be in trouble or something!"

Boy, are you ever *powerful*!

NOTES & CREDITS

"Productivity and the Academic 'Business'" was adapted from *Productivity and Higher Education* © 1992 by Peterson's Guides, Inc., Princeton, NJ. With permission. Available by calling 1-800-338-3282 or via petersons.com.

"The Death and Rebirth of Empathy" was adapted from a somewhat longer version that originally appeared in the October 1994 issue of *Trusteeship*, Association of Governing Boards of Universities and Colleges.

The following selections originally appeared in a somewhat different form in *Speaking His Mind: Five Years of Commentaries on Higher Education* by Stephen Joel Trachtenberg, Oryx Press, 1994:

—"Searching for Perspective in a De-Controlled World."

—"The Importance of Ancient History."

—"Why It Matters How We Cut the Cake" (previously titled "The Beginning of Wisdom").

The selection credited in "Short Takes I" to *Connection*, New England Board of Higher Education, Summer 1988, was excerpted and edited from the original article.

The selection credited in "Short Takes III" to *Academe,* American Association of University Professors, January-February 1996, was excerpted and edited from the original article.

The selections credited to the following sources in "Short Takes I-IV" were excerpted and edited from speeches originally appearing in *Speaking His Mind: Five Years of Commentaries on Higher Education* by Stephen Joel Trachtenberg, Oryx Press, 1994:

—Remarks at the Inauguration of Stephen Joel Trachtenberg as 15th President of The George Washington University, April 16, 1989.

—Remarks at *The New York Times* Presidents Forum, New York City, November 22, 1991.

—"The Difficult Quest for Balance in American Higher Education," *The World & I*, The Washington Times Corporation, December 1991.

—Remarks at the Mitre Corporation's "Distinguished Lecture Series," Bedford, Mass., February 25, 1992.

—Remarks at the 27th Annual Conference, Society for College and University Planning, Minneapolis, Minn., August 3, 1992.

—Remarks at the Mid-Atlantic Convention, Society for College and University Planning, Baltimore, April 15, 1993.

—Remarks at the D.C. Jewish Community Center's John R. Risher Public Affairs Forum, Washington, D.C., May 6, 1993.

—Remarks at the X Triennial Conference, International Association of University Presidents, Kobe, Japan, July 1993.